Precedence, Titles, and Forms
of Address in Canada

PRECEDENCE, TITLES, AND FORMS OF ADDRESS IN CANADA

Peter W Noonan B.A. (Windsor) LL.B. (Windsor)

Of Osgoode Hall, Barrister-at-Law and Solicitor of the

Superior Court of Ontario; Notary Public in and for

the Province of Ontario

MAGISTRALIS

Ottawa, Canada

Precedence, Titles, and Forms of Address in Canada

Copyright © by Peter W. Noonan.

All Rights Reserved.

ISBN 978-1-7780030-6-6 (hardcover)

Cataloging in Publication Data may be obtained from:

Library and Archives Canada

395 Wellington St, Ottawa, ON

Canada K1A 0N4

CONTENTS

TABLE OF CASES

TABLE OF STATUTES AND INSTRUMENTS

Provincial Statutes

INTRODUCTION

Precedence is an order of things. When applied to individuals it determines who is placed first and subsequent in society, in government, in a place, or on an occasion. A legal dictionary defines precedence as "The act or state of going before; adjustment of place. The right of being first placed in a certain order".[1] Precedence is a necessary corollary to the establishment of order in a political society. It is essential to the purposes of state protocol, and every state relies upon the concept of precedence to establish its authority.

The importance of precedency to the subject of state protocol cannot be underestimated. Protocol is the rules of etiquette established by state authorities that are observed at state ceremonies. As one specialist stated to a parliamentary committee, "The fundamentals [of protocol] are always the same because everything comes back to the fact that it's based on precedence."[2]

As Canada is a federal state the rules of precedence can become a fertile field for disputes between the Federal government and its provincial counterparts. As one provincial specialist has stated: "I don't think there's a month that goes by where there's not a disagreement between communications staff at a provin-

---

1. Blacks Law Dictionary, 4th ed. rev. West Publishing Company, St. Paul (Minn.), 1968.

2. Report of the Standing Committee on Canadian Heritage, *Review of National Protocol Procedures*, 41st Parliament, 1st Session, October 2012, remarks made by Elizabeth Rody, Chief of Protocol and Director of Events at International and Inter-parliamentary Affairs of the Parliament of Canada, p. 4

cial level and a federal level with regard to a federal news release or a federal-provincial event."[3]

Nor is it likely that a satisfactory way could be found to militate against the eruption of precedent disputes in a federal state. As one federal official has stated: ". . . it would be very difficult to come up with a national framework for something like this, partly because people are very jealous of their territory."[4]

As such, the focus of this monograph will be on the concept of the relative precedence of official actors within the framework of the Canadian state. International, ecclesiastical, and private organizations may have their own systems of precedence but they are outside the scope of this work.

3. Ibid, p. 17, remarks made by Dwight MacAulay, Chief of Protocol, Executive Council

4. Ibid, remarks made by Audrey O'Brien, Clerk of the House of Commons

PART I.

_____

PART ONE - THE LAW OF PRECEDENCE IN CANADA

_____

CHAPTER 1.

THE LEGAL FOUNDATION OF PRECEDENCE IN THE COMMON LAW

In a constitutional monarchy such as Canada, precedency emanates from the Crown or, more particularly, from the Sovereign as part of the royal prerogative.[1] As a monarchy, it follows that all grades of precedence for individuals will be established in relation to their position vis-a-vis the monarch. Thus the Sovereign, or his or her lawful delegate, will determine the relative precedence of individuals who are variously employed by, subservient to, or supportive of the state structure. Accordingly, as the precedence granted to individuals in Canada results from an exercise of the royal prerogative, precedence is a matter of law.

That precedence could be and is a matter of law has long been established in English jurisprudence, which forms the legal inheritance that Canada received through the process of colonisation. English law remains the bedrock of the public law of Canada, and the powers of the royal prerogative form part of our public law that was received from England during the formative days of the European settlement in what we now know as Canada.

The earliest acknowledgement of precedence as a subject that was cognizable by the laws of England comes to us in the case of *Ashton v Jennings* (1674), 3 Keble 462; 2 Lev 133 (KB) a decision of the Court of King's Bench in England in which a Mrs.

1. Paul Lordon Q.C., *Crown Law*, Butterworths, Toronto and Vancouver, 1991, p. 102.

Ashton, the wife of a doctor of divinity at Cambridge University, insisted on being given a placement at a funeral that was more prominent than that of a Mrs. Jennings, the wife of a Justice of the Peace. Jennings proceeded to push Ashton out of her place of prominence because she, Jennings, held higher precedence than Ashton. Ashton sued for battery as a result of her displacement at the funeral. Judgement was given to the plaintiff, Ashton, but only because Jennings did make a judicial admission in her pleadings that Ashton had been forcibly removed from her place of prominence.

Ashton v *Jennings* is important because the Court of King's Bench accepted as a matter of principle that precedence was a subject matter that the laws of England would recognize and adjudicate upon. However, the Court took pains to decide that the jurisdiction to adjudicate upon claims of precedence lay outside the Court of King's Bench, but lay, rather, with a very curious English court known as the Court of Chivalry, whose procedures were governed by civil law, rather than by English common law. A few years later in another case, *R* v *Parker* (1688), 2 Keble 316 (KB) the court had recognized what it called the law of the Constable and the Marshal (i.e. chivalry) as a separate part of the laws of England.

Both *Ashton* v *Jennings* and *R* v *Parker* were in accord with the earlier views expressed by Lord Coke, as Chief Justice of the Court of King's Bench, in the early years of the seventeenth century. In *Poole and Redhead's Case* (1614), 1 Rolle 87 (KB) Lord Coke dealt with a case concerning the payment of the fees owed to the King upon the grant of a knighthood. Lord Coke stated that the common law courts had no jurisdiction in the matter and opined in *obiter dicta* that jurisdiction in such matters lay with the Court of the Constable and the Marshal, which, in those times, was another way of acknowledging the Court of Chivalry. As part of his dictum in that case Lord Coke cited precedence as one of the matters that lay outside the realm of the common law courts and as one matter lying within the jurisdiction of the Court of Chivalry.

However, subsequent and diligent research by scholars into the records of the obscure Court of Chivalry has disclosed that the Court of Chivalry never actually heard a case of precedence, and the substance of its jurisdiction was focused on the improper use of coats of arms granted by the King or Queen. The Court of Chivalry was (and is) an ancient court that has sat only intermittently and it has sometimes fallen into abeyance for long periods, which accounts perhaps for the fact that its apparent lack of cases concerning precedence was not generally known to common law judges and lawyers of the seventeenth century. That confusion was exacerbated by the fact that the high royal official known as the Earl Marshal among his many other duties presided at the Court of Chivalry in chivalric cases (occasionally in conjunction with another high official, the Constable of England) and the Earl Marshal, or subsequently the commissioners who were appointed to exercise his office when the position of the Earl Marshal was vacant, did separately hear and decide disputes over precedence in proceedings that offered the participants some degree of procedural fairness.[2]

It therefore seems likely that both Lord Coke, and subsequent justices of the Court of King's Bench, misapprehended the separate jurisdictions involving the Earl Marshal of England (and sometimes also the Constable of England). One jurisdiction was (and is) the Court of Chivalry, which is a judicial body, and the other jurisdiction was a separate executive decision-

2. As an example, on March 29, 1609, a "Marshal's Court" was convened to resolve a dispute over the precedence of Sir Thomas Smith resulting in a decision that Sir Thomas Smith, an ex-ambassador to Russia, was held to have precedence over those Knights Bachelor of the City of London who had been knighted previous to him because Sir Thomas Smith had had the honour "to stand covered in the presence of a king." (G.D. Squibb, *The High Court of Chivalry, A study of the Civil Law in England*, Clarendon Press, Oxford, 1959 at p. 33

making function involving questions of precedence that were vested exclusively in the Earl Marshal or perhaps the Earl Marshal and the Constable together. Both jurisdictions were conflated in the jurisprudence and legal writings of the seventeenth century with the result that today the common law courts in England deny any jurisdiction over precedence in favour of the obscure Court of Chivalry, which last sat in the mid-twentieth century.[3][4]

From the above one may conclude, from a Canadian perspective, that firstly the common law courts recognized that precedence was a matter of law, and secondly, the early English jurisprudence that found jurisdiction over precedence to be outside the scope of the common law appears to have been in error. As such, it follows that a dispute over precedence in Canada, where the specialized Court of Chivalry was never established, should be within the jurisdiction of the ordinary common law courts.

3. *Manchester Corporation* v *Manchester Palace of Varieties Ltd.*, [1955] P. 133; 1 All ER 387(Ct. Chiv.); *Sabha* v *Attorney General*, [2009] 4 LRC 818 (Trinidad and Tobago, P.C.) at 836 per Lord Mance.

4. This matter is fully developed in G. D. Squibb, *Precedence in England and Wales*, Clarendon Press, Oxford, 1981 at pp 90-93

CHAPTER 2.

THE EARLY ENGLISH TABLES OF PRECEDENCE

In the early centuries of the English kingdom precedence was generally focussed on social precedence rather than official precedence. Several precedential orders were issued with perhaps varying degrees of official sanction. Often those early orders of precedence were made in expectation of the forthcoming coronation of a new monarch. The relative precedence of nobles in relation to the King or Queen was all important to the English elite in the earliest eras of the kingdom. A very early example, and perhaps the first attempt at a comprehensive order of precedence was *The Order of all Estates of Nobles and Gentry of England*, dated October 8, 1399, which laid out an order of precedence in executive form in preparation for the coronation of King Henry IV of England. However, the original of that Order has been lost and it is now known only from copies. Nor was it an official document issued by the Crown. Rather, it appears to have been a private compilation. Nevertheless, it did provide an initial framework for English precedence and it was subsequently relied upon when official orders of precedence were developed later in England.

An important subsequent example, and one that was clearly an official act of the Crown, was the *Order of all States of Worship and Gentry of England*, dated November 6, 1429, and issued jointly by the Duke of Bedford in his capacity as the Constable of England, and by the Duke of Norfolk in his capacity as the Earl Marshal of the realm, in preparation for the coronation of King Henry VI of England. That table generally parallelled the earlier, unofficial 1399 Order, and in the 1429 Order, one can see that precedence is provided for 25 grades of nobility, gentry, and officialdom, including places for the officers of the Royal Household and the most important royal officials.

However, perhaps the most important of the English tables of precedence issued in the medieval period was done in preparation for an important state dinner in 1520, and entitled *Precedence of Great Estates in their own degrees*. That comprehensive order became the basis for a table subsequently issued by the Commissioners for exercising the office of the Earl Marshal during the reign of Queen Elizabeth I. The table prepared for the Queen was issued as an ordinance, giving it a formal legal effectiveness, and with many subsequent changes it provided the foundation for the modern tables of precedence in Britain and influenced the development of tables of precedence in the Commonwealth realms.

The early English tables were concerned to a large extent with the relative rankings of the classes of nobility and gentry in England, and their interrelationship with the high ecclesiastical authorities whose precedence in pre-reformation days had been separately established by the authority of the Pope in Rome. After the protestant reformation, tables of precedence were established that combined the secular and ecclesiastical authorities, as the monarch thereafter reigned over both church and state in England. That process began with legislation in the form of the *House of Lords Precedence Act 1539*[1]. In that Act the King in Parliament for the first time prescribed precedence for both layman and ecclesiastical figures. Although the former dual precedence of layman and ecclesiastics was maintained in the Act it was only a matter of time before a consolidated table was crafted for both lay and ecclesiastical officials. The Act is also important because it placed officers of state in an order

---

1. 31 Hen. VIII, c.10

of precedence and made that precedence applicable outside as well as inside the House of Lords.[2]

An important element of distinction between precedence in Great Britain and precedence in the overseas British empire was the fact that the nobility of Britain played an important role in the government of the kingdom. The nobility, at least its male members, served in the House of Lords, the upper chamber of the British Parliament and therefore they had both a social status and an official status within the kingdom. Thus it was essential to place the relative ranks of the high nobility, the aristocracy, and the lesser nobility, the gentry, in an order of precedence together with the highest officials of the kingdom and the most senior ecclesiastical authorities belonging to the state church in the kingdom.

The result is the following modern precedential ranks (displayed here in a very abbreviated form):

<u>Royalty and Nobility</u>

• Royal Family
• The Archbishops and the high officers of state
• Dukes/Duchesses
• Marquises/Marquiseses[3]
• Eldest sons of Dukes
• Earls/Countesses
• Eldest sons of Marquises
• Younger sons of Dukes
• Viscounts/Viscountesses
• Eldest sons of Earls
• Younger sons of Marquises

---

2. Squibb, Precedence, p. 24

3. This is the preferred spelling in Canadian English (see *The Houghton Mifflin Canadian Dictionary of the English Language*, Houghton Mifflin Canada Limited, Markham (Ont.), 1982

- Bishops
- Baron/Baroness & Lords/Ladies (Scottish)

<u>The Gentry</u>

- Master of the Rolls and Justices of the Supreme Court
- Royal Household officers
- The Ministry and certain children of Earls, Viscounts and Barons
- Members of the Order of the Garter and the Order of the Thistle
- Privy Councillors
- Senior Judges and certain children of Viscounts and Barons
- Baronets
- Knights/Dames
- Lower court judges
- Esquires
- Gentlemen/Gentlewomen

Because precedence was established in England and then in Great Britain based upon social classifications in a society where titles of nobility passed through male primogeniture the precedence of women was ranked separately from men and then for the most part as a derivative of their husband's or father's social rank. This separate precedence between males and females continues today in the United Kingdom and it applies to the Royal Family[4] as well as to the ranks of British nobility.

4. Except for the Sovereign.

CHAPTER 3.

THE PRECEDENCE OF THE ROYAL FAMILY

The precedence of the Royal Family for Canadian purposes is determined in the United Kingdom and is subject to the decisions of the Sovereign. Currently, the accepted precedence is as follows:

MALES

1. The sovereign, whether male or female

2. The sovereign's eldest son

3. The sovereign's younger sons[1]

4. The sovereign's grandsons[2]

5. The sovereign's brothers[3]

6. The sovereign's uncles

7. The sovereign's nephews

8. The sovereign's (male) cousins

FEMALES

1. The sovereign, whether male or female.

2. Queen Consort

1. Ordered according to their birth.
2. Ordered according to the rules of primogeniture.
3. Ordered according to their birth..

3. Queens Dowager

4. The wife of the sovereign's eldest son

5. Wives of the sovereign's younger sons[4]

6. The sovereign's daughters[5]

7. Wives of the sovereign's grandsons[6]

8. The sovereign's granddaughters[7]

9. Wives of the sovereign's brothers[8]

10. The sovereign's sisters[9]

11. Wives of the sovereign's uncles[10]

12. The sovereign's aunts[11]

13. Wives of the sovereign's nephews[12]

14. The sovereign's nieces[13]

15. Wives of the sovereign's (male) cousins[14]

---

4. Ordered according to their spouses' precedence.
5. Ordered according to their birth.
6. Ordered according to their spouses' precedence.
7. Ordered according to the rules of primogeniture.
8. Ordered according to their spouses' precedence.
9. Ordered according to their birth.
10. Ordered according to their spouses' precedence.
11. Ordered according to their birth. These are the sisters of the Sovereign's parents.
12. Ordered according to their spouses' precedence.
13. Ordered according to the rules of primogeniture.
14. Ordered according to their spouses' precedence.

16. The sovereign's (female) cousins[15]

15. Ordered according to the rules of primogeniture.

CHAPTER 4.

PRECEDENCE IN THE AMERICAS

In New France, the society established by French colonization was very much a hierarchical society with an established state church in the form of the Roman Catholic church. In absolutist France precedence was always a matter of the King's prerogative. As the representative of the King the Governor of New France had the highest precedence, followed by the Intendant and the Bishop. The priesthood was prominent in all of the local communities and even had a role to play within the state, as initially, it was the priests who conveyed the terms of any new ordinances or proclamations from the government to the people. Also prominent in the local society were the local militia captain, and the Seigneurs, who were a type of feudal landholding lord who was owed dues from the people that farmed within a Seigneury. Occupying the lowest rung on the social ladder in New France were the habitants, the class of people who were mainly concerned with farming or artisan work. The conquest of Canada in 1759-60, and the subsequent transfer of sovereignty over Canada from France to Great Britain by the Treaty of Paris in 1763, overturned the social and political structures of New France with the departure of the colonial elites, who returned to France, and by the consequent reorganization of the state along British colonial lines. Any order of precedence for the colony flowing from the King in Paris was washed away by the conquest. Thereafter it was British forms of precedence that were applied throughout Canada.

In British America, there were few, if any, members of the nobility who fell within the ranks of the aristocracy, other than the occasional governors drawn from the English, Scottish, or Irish nobility. Furthermore, the state churches in Great Britain never became fully established in North America and, in any event, remained mere outposts of the metropolitan churches before ultimately acquiring their autonomy. As a result, precedence in the Americas was from the inception of the colonies largely confined to official ranks and reflected social status only to the extent that British subjects of a certain social prominence were commonly appointed to important official positions. Hereditary ranks, in general, were given no recognition in the Orders of Precedence established in the North American colonies.

Interestingly, one unofficial attempt was made to order social precedence in the Americas. John Edmunson, the Mowbray Herald in the College of Arms in London apparently crafted an order of precedence for colonial society in the Americas in the late seventeenth century. A copy of his attempt is contained in a work by Anthony Stokes entitled *A View of the Constitution of the British Colonies in North-America and the West Indies*. Edmunson's attempt at colonial social precedence was unofficial and it remains uncertain whether it was followed in North America but it does illustrate the thoughts current during the period concerning colonial precedency. Edmunson's table was chiefly concerned with the gentry in the Americas and so he did not attempt to integrate peers into his order of precedence. Curiously, he included baronets, a type of hereditary knighthood but did not create a place for knights. Perhaps Edmunson was thinking of the Baronets of Nova Scotia, an ostensibly Canadian dignity that is in reality Scottish (although originally having a Canadian purpose). Herewith is the order compiled by Edmunson:

Rules of Precedence Compared and Adjusted from the several Acts and Statutes made and provided in England, for

the Settlement of the Precedence of Men and Women in America, Joseph Edmunson, Mowbray Herald[1]

1. Governor of the Province and His Wife

2. Lieutenant Governor and His Wife

3. President of the [Provincial] Council and His Wife

4. Members of His Majesty's [Provincial] Council and their Wives

5. The Speaker of the Commons House of Assembly and his Wife

6. The Chief Justice [of the Province]

7. The Treasurer [of the Province] and his Wife

8. The Associate Judges [of the Provincial Court] and their Wives

9. Baronets and their Wives

10. His Majesty's Attorney General [for the Province] and his Wife

11. The Judge of the [Vice-] Admiralty [Court for the Province] and his Wife

12. The Secretary of the Province and His Wife

13. Members of the Commons House of Assembly and their Wives*

14. The Mayor[s?] and his wife

---

1. Published in Anthony Stokes, *A View of the Constitution of the British Colonies in North-America and the West Indies*, Anthony Stokes, London, 1783, pp. 201-02, Kindle edition.

15. Aldermen and their Wives

16. Members of the [Proprietary] Corporation and their Wives

* The Members of the Assembly, Crown Officers, etc., of any particular Province, have no other rank out of their Province, than what belongs to them in their private capacity as men. The Widow of a late Governor has not any precedence as such. A Governor of one Province, or his wife, coming into another Province, have not, in that Province where they visit, any precedence above their rank in private life.

In the imperial possessions held by Britain in the Americas,[2] Precedence was always dealt with as a function of the executive government, and any disputes over precedence were resolved by executive decision-making, albeit with some degree of procedural fairness to those concerned. Unlike Britain, where precedency was rooted in social conditions and classes and was therefore personal, in the Americas there was almost no indigenous nobility, and titled persons in the colonies were almost invariably civil or military officials sent out from Britain. There was an untitled landed gentry that was wealth-based but no definitive precedency attached to the gentry other than perhaps the ambiguous rankings of esquires and gentlemen for which there was even in England no real precedency outside of the lesser sons of the nobility.[3]

Rather, in the Americas precedency was attached to official appointments and not to social class. Nevertheless, its importance was not lessened by the absence in the Americas of any markers of social class distinctions. At the apex of the colonial

2. The territories that became Canada only gradually came under British rule: Newfoundland from 1583-1638, Rupert's Land, 1670, Nova Scotia, 1713, Cape Breton 1758, New France, 1760.

3. But in Lower Canada (later Quebec) there was a titled class of gentry in the form of the Seigneur. A Seigneur was a man of substantial landholding wealth who was owed deference and even some quasi-feudal rights by his tenants.

social structure stood the Governor of a colony and his wife. No matter how lowly their status and precedence may have been in the realm of England, in the Americas, the Governor and his wife outranked all persons in the official (and social) hierarchy because of the Governor's position as the representative of the King in the colonial province.

In the colonial hierarchy, the next most important officials in the provinces were the members of the Provincial Council. The Provincial Council was the colonial counterpart of the Privy Council in Britain, which collectively served (and continues to serve) as the constitutional advisor to the Sovereign. Like the Privy Council, therefore, the Provincial Council served as the primary constitutional advisor to the Governor of a colonial province. And that was not the only similarity. While the Privy Council in Britain served as a final court of appeal for legal causes arising abroad in the empire (and in a few minor domestic causes) in a colonial province the highest level of appellate court for all legal causes was the Provincial Council. Finally, unlike the Privy Council in Britain, a Provincial Council also served as the upper house of a colonial legislature. Thus, a Provincial Council exercised executive, judicial, and legislative functions, giving it paramount influence in the life of a colony.

Given the importance of a Provincial Council (later re-fashioned in Canada into the provincial Legislative Councils), it was important to appoint to it men of substantial achievement in colonial society, and thus members of the provincial elites were commonly appointed either through a recommendation to the Board of Trade in Britain from a colonial governor, or directly by the Board of Trade based on their knowledge of particular colonial societies. In circumstances where the number of active councillors fell below seven a provincial governor could make appointments to his council to bring the number of councillors up to seven but the governor's appointees were subject to confirmation (or revocation) by the Board of Trade. Where a governor's appointment of a councillor was revoked, that revocation did not affect the validity of the former incumbent's official acts while they were awaiting the decision of the Board of Trade on their appointment.

Precedence was important to Provincial Councillors because, in the absence, incapacity, or death of both the governor and the lieutenant governor (if there was one) the administration of the province would fall to the senior member of the Provincial Council, who would serve as president of the Council until a new governor or lieutenant-governor could be appointed and take up residence in the colony.

For the most part disputes over the precedence of provincial councillors arose in one of two ways. In the first place, a new member may have delayed presenting himself to be sworn into the Council and subsequently, a man appointed later may have been sworn in before him. The second way that precedence disputes arose resulted from a governor making a temporary appointment to the Provincial Council when the number of councillors fell below seven. In that circumstance, someone might have taken up their appointment before the person whose actual appointment by the Board of Trade pre-dated the Governor's appointee but who was delayed in transit in assuming their position.[4]

Thus, precedence in the Provincial Council in at least some provinces seems to have been determined by the date that an appointee was actually sworn into office. A clear example of how that could lead to a dispute occurred in colonial Virginia. There, an issue arose concerning whether the date of first appointment was the date shown upon the appointing instrument issued by the Crown, or the date that a member was first

4. In one notable instance in 1766 a member of the Barbados Council refused to take his place on the island's Council when he learned that the Governor had made a temporary appointment of the Governor's son-in-law to the Council and that the 'royal' appointee would thus have to concede precedence to the governor's son-in-law. (Infra, LeBaree, *Royal Government in America*, p. 146.)

sworn into the Council. The practice in Virginia was to date an appointment of a Councillor from the date that he took the oath of office as a member. When an issue concerning the respective precedence of two councillors arose as a result of this practice advice was sought from the Board of Trade in London. The Board considered the matter and advised the King that it had "been the general custom for the members of your Majesty's councils in the several colonies and plantations in America to take place according to the date of the royal mandamus[5] whereby they are appointed."[6] The King approved an Order-in-Council to that effect. The Governor responded to the Board of Trade that the Order-in-Council was contrary to the customs of Virginia but the Board of Trade refused to consider any other method for determining precedency other than the date on the appointing instrument.

Another problem of precedence arose when an individual held an appointment and then surrendered it only to be subsequently reappointed again to the Provincial Council at a much later date. The question that arose there was whether his precedence should be based on his expired first appointment or only on his most recent appointment. The practice of the Board of Trade on this point varied. For the most part, the date of the second appointment was taken as the date from which to determine precedence but there were exceptions to that, and some individuals were permitted to trace their precedence from the date of an earlier appointment.

Although a colonial governor held precedence over both civilian as well as military officials in a British colony that changed

---

5. This instrument was apparently a form of Letters Close, being royal letters signed at the top by the King with his sign manual and initialled by him at the bottom or countersigned by a Secretary of State and then folded to conceal the contents. The royal signet was fixed with wax to hold the folds together.

6. Leonard Woods LaBaree Ph.d., *Royal Government in America; A Study of the British Colonial System Before 1783*, Yale University Press, New Haven, 1930., at 145.

in the Americas beginning around 1755 when the Seven Years War began. From that year onwards there was invariably a British Army Commander-in-Chief resident in the Americas and that officer was able to establish his precedence over the colonial governors in all matters concerning the military.[7] However, the colonial governors retained their authority over civilian matters within their respective colonies.

To formalize the new precedence relationships in the Americas the King issued a Table of Precedence for the British possessions in the Americas under his royal sign manual dated December 17, 1760. Following upon the *Capitulations* signed by Governor General Vaudreuil and the British commander, General Jeffrey Amherst on September 8, 1760, at Montreal, this Table of Precedence was the first to apply to all of the territories that later became Canada.

Table of Precedence for the Military Service in America[8]

December 17, 1760

1. Commander in chief of the British forces

2. Royal Governors when in their respective provinces

3. General officers on the staff

4. Royal Governors when out of their respective provinces

5. Lieutenant governors and presidents of councils when acting [as] governors in their respective provinces

6. Colonels

---

7. The colonial governors never had any authority over the ships and establishments of the Royal Navy, although they did have some supervisory jurisdiction over vice-admiralty courts.

8. LaBaree, *Royal Government in America*, p. 109.

7. Lieutenant governors and presidents of councils when acting [as] governors but out of their respective provinces

8. Lieutenant governors when not acting governors but in their respective provinces

9. Lieutenant governors when not acting governors and out of their respective provinces

10. Governors of charter colonies when in their respective colonies

11. All field officers under the rank of colonel

12. Lieutenant governors of proprietary governments when out of their respective provinces

13. Governors of charter colonies when out of their respective colonies

N.B. All royal governors and lieutenant governors and all proprietary lieutenant governors were to take rank within their respective grades according to the dates of their commissions, but governors of charter colonies according to the dates of their charters.

After the outbreak of the Revolutionary War and the Battle of Bunker Hill in 1775, the British Commander in Chief in the Americas, General Gage, was recalled to Britain and subsequently, the command of British forces in North America was split, with Gage's successor, General Howe, made the Commander in Chief in of the British Forces in rebellious America while Major General Guy Carleton headquartered in Quebec City received an appointment as Commander in Chief of British Forces in Canada. After the end of the American Revolutionary War (1775-1783), the title of commander in chief was usually accorded to the Governor General of British North America located at Quebec City, although more junior general officers were usually assigned to command the actual British and Canadian troops in the field during wartime.

CHAPTER 5.

PRECEDENCE IN POST-CONFEDERATION CANADA

After the confederation of the British North American provinces into the new state of Canada in 1867, a new table of precedence for officials encompassing the country as a whole became necessary. Consequently, a new table of precedence for Canada was devised and approved by Queen Victoria under the royal sign manual on July 23, 1868, and subsequently published in the government gazette. The 1868 table of precedence still forms the basis of the table of precedence established for Canada in the twenty-first century.

Dominion of Canada Table of Precedence

July 23, 1868

1 The governor-general, or officer administering the government

2 The senior officer in command of the troops, if of the rank of general, and the officer in command of Her Majesty's naval forces on the station, if of the rank of an admiral, their own relative rank being determined by the queen's regulations on that subject.

3 The Lieutenant Governor of Ontario

4 The Lieutenant Governor of Quebec

5 The Lieutenant Governor of Nova Scotia

6 The Lieutenant Governor of New Brunswick

7 The Archbishop and Bishops according to seniority[1]

8 Members of the Cabinet, according to seniority[2][3]

9 The Speaker of the Senate

10 The chief judges of the courts of law and equity, according to seniority[4][5][6][7]

1. Meaning seniority determined by the date of their consecration without regard to their religious denomination. This placed both Anglican and other protestant denominations together with Roman Catholic bishops, in a common ranking.

2. This was a special precedence granted to Canadian Ministers and was based upon the fact that Canadian Ministers were all summoned to be members of the Queen's Privy Council for Canada placing them on the same level as British Ministers who were likewise summoned to be members of the Privy Council of the United Kingdom upon taking office. (The creation of a separate privy council for Canada was unique in the evolution of British possessions. In other dominions such as Australia or New Zealand there was no Privy Council but colonial statesmen from all of the more important colonies (including Canada) were often summoned to be members of the Imperial Privy Council in the United Kingdom.) In Great Britain, the members of the Privy Council of the United Kingdom held precedence over other public officers, except the Lord Chancellor.

3. In keeping with the practices of Westminster-style governments of this period there was no separate precedence granted to the Prime Minister of the country. That, however, would change as political structures evolved in Canada in the twentieth century and the office of Prime Minister became constitutionally recognized.

4. In the new Dominion of Canada the judges of all of the superior courts were now to be placed on a common list of precedence according to their dates of appointment.

5. At confederation in 1867 and for several years afterward there was no Supreme Court of Canada and that is why there is no reference to a Chief Justice of Canada in the original Table of Precedence for Canada.

6. In a despatch from the Secretary of State for the colonies, Sir M. Hicks-Beach, dated October 31, 1878, a decision made by Governor General Lord Dufferin assigning precedence for the judges of the Supreme Court of Canada immediately after the Speaker of the Senate was noted with approval.

7. A despatch from the Colonial Office dated November 3, 1879, authorized the

11 Members of the privy council not of the cabinet[8]

12 General officers of Her Majesty's army serving in the dominion, and officers of the rank of admiral in the royal navy, serving on the British North American station, not being in the chief command; the relative rank of such officers to be determined by the queen's regulations [9] [10]

13 The senior officer in command of the troops, if of the rank of colonel or lieutenant colonel, and the officer in command of her Majesty's naval forces on the station, if of equivalent rank; their own relative rank being determined by the queen's regulations[11]

14 Members of the Senate

15 Speaker of the House of Commons

16 Puisne Judges of the courts of law and equity according to seniority.

17 Members of the House of Commons

Chief Justices of the provincial courts of law and equity to rank immediately after the Chief Justice of Canada and the puisne justices of the Supreme Court of Canada to rank next after and before the puisne justices of the various provincial superior courts of law and equity. The puisne Justices of the Supreme Court of Canada thereafter followed the Speaker of the House of Commons and thus preceded the puisne Justices of the provincial superior courts of law and equity.

8. Membership in the Queen's (or King's) Privy Council for Canada is for life. Those outside of the Cabinet are usually retired politicians but there may be others. For instance, each Chief Justice of Canada is traditionally summoned to become a member of the Privy Council.

9. Officers of the Canadian militia were subordinated to their regular British Army counterparts under the *Militia Act*.

10. A Circular Despatch from the Secretary of State for the Colonies dated March 17, 1879 provided that officers in an acting role were to be accorded the precedence that attached to their acting rank rather than their substantive rank.

11. This would apply to officers serving in the dominion.

18 Members of the Executive Council, within their province[12]

19 Speaker of the Legislative Council, within his province[13]

20 Members of the Legislative Council, within their province[14]

21 Speaker of the Legislative Assembly, within his province

22 Members of the Legislative Assembly, within their province

---

In the years following, the Table of Precedence for Canada underwent changes and revisions as the British presence in Canada diminished, and Canada evolved into the modern independent sovereign state that it has become.

12. The Executive Council consists of the Ministers of the Crown for the time being within a provincial government. It serves as the provincial counterpart to the federal Privy Council, though less august in stature.

13. In the early period of Canadian government following confederation the provincial legislatures were bicameral legislatures and the Legislative Council constituted the upper house of the provincial legislature. All provinces have since abolished their respective legislative councils.

14. In the early period of Canadian government following confederation the provincial legislatures were bicameral legislatures and the Legislative Council constituted the upper house of the provincial legislature. All provinces have since abolished their respective legislative councils.

CHAPTER 6.

THE MODERN TABLE OF PRECEDENCE FOR CANADA

The Crown continues to promulgate a current Table of Precedence for Canada from time to time. Now, near the end of the first quarter of the twenty-first century, the Table of Precedence for Canada stands in the following order:

Table of Precedence for Canada[1]

As revised on July 3, 2015 *

1. The Governor General of Canada or the Administrator of the Government of Canada [1] [1.1] [2] [2.1]

2. The Prime Minister of Canada[3]

3. The Chief Justice of Canada[4]

4. The Speaker of the Senate

5. The Speaker of the House of Commons

6. Ambassadors, High Commissioners, Ministers Plenipotentiary[5]

7. Members of the Canadian Ministry:
a. Members of the Cabinet; and
b. Ministers of State;
with relative precedence within sub-categories (a) and (b) gov-

---

1. https://www.canada.ca/en/canadian-heritage/services/ protocol-guidelines-special-event/table-precedence-canada.html [accessed July 28, 2024].

erned by the date of their appointment to the King's Privy Council for Canada.

8. The Leader of the Opposition[3]

9. The Lieutenant Governor of Ontario

The Lieutenant Governor of Quebec

The Lieutenant Governor of Nova Scotia

The Lieutenant Governor of New Brunswick

The Lieutenant Governor of Manitoba

The Lieutenant Governor of British Columbia

The Lieutenant Governor of Prince Edward Island

The Lieutenant Governor of Saskatchewan

The Lieutenant Governor of Alberta

The Lieutenant Governor of Newfoundland and Labrador[6]

10. Members of the King's Privy Council for Canada, not of the Canadian Ministry, in accordance with the date of their appointment to the Privy Council but with precedence given to those who bear the honorary title "Right Honourable" in accordance with the date of receiving the honorary title.

11. Premiers of the Provinces of Canada in the same order as Lieutenant Governors[6]

12. The Commissioner of the Northwest Territories

The Commissioner of the Yukon Territory

The Commissioner of Nunavut[7]

13. Premiers of the Territories of Canada in the same order as Commissioners [7]

14. Representatives of faith communities[8]

15. Puisne Judges of the Supreme Court of Canada

16. The Chief Justice and the Associate Chief Justice of the Federal Court of Canada

17. a. Chief Justices of the highest court of each Province and Territory; and
b. Chief Justices and Associate Chief Justices of the other superior courts of the Provinces and Territories;

with precedence within sub-categories (a) and (b) governed by the date of appointment as Chief Justice

18. a. Judges of the Federal Court of Canada;
b. Puisne Judges of the superior courts of the Provinces and Territories;
c. The Chief Judge of the Tax Court of Canada;
d. The Associate Chief Judge of the Tax Court of Canada; and
e. Judges of the Tax Court of Canada; with precedence within each sub-category governed by the date of appointment

19. Senators of Canada

20. Members of the House of Commons

21. Consuls General of countries without diplomatic representation

22. Clerk of the Privy Council and Secretary to Cabinet

23. The Chief of the Defence Staff and the Commissioner of the Royal Canadian Mounted Police[9]

24. Speakers of Legislative Assemblies, within their Province and Territory

25. Members of Executive Councils, within their Province and Territory

26. Judges of Provincial and Territorial Courts, within their Province and Territory

27. Members of Legislative Assemblies, within their Province and Territory

28. Chairperson of the Canadian Association of Former Parliamentarians

Notes

* The terminology found in this table was updated following His Majesty King Charles III's accession to the Throne on September 8, 2022.

[1] The presence of the Sovereign in Canada does not impair or supersede the authority of the Governor General to perform the functions delegated to him under the *Letters Patent constituting the office of the Governor General [of Canada].*[2] The Governor General, under all circumstances, should be accorded precedence immediately after the Sovereign.

[1.1]In the absence of the Governor General of Canada and the Administrator of the Government of Canada, precedence to be given immediately after the Prime Minister of Canada to the Lieutenant Governor of the province in which the ceremony or occasion takes place.

[2] Precedence to be given immediately after the Chief Justice of Canada to former Governors General, with relative precedence among them governed by the date of their leaving office.

[2.1] Precedence to be given immediately after the former Governors-General to surviving spouses of deceased former Governors-General (applicable only where the spouse was married to the Governor General during the latter's term of office), with relative precedence among them governed by the dates on which the deceased former Governors General left office.

[3] Precedence to be given immediately after the surviving spouses of deceased former Governors General referred to in Note 2.1 to former Prime Ministers, with relative precedence among them governed by the dates of their first assumption of office.

[4] Precedence to be given immediately after former Prime Ministers to former Chief Justices of Canada, with relative precedence among them governed by the dates of their appointment as Chief Justice of Canada.

[5] Precedence among Ambassadors and High Commissioners, who rank equally, to be determined by the date of the presentation of their credentials. Precedence to be given to Chargés d'Affaires immediately after Ministers Plenipotentiary.

[6] This provision does not apply to such ceremonies and occasions which are of a provincial nature.

[7] This provision does not apply to such ceremonies and occasions which are of a territorial nature.

[8]The religious dignitaries will be senior Canadian representatives of faith communities having a significant presence in a relevant jurisdiction. The relative precedence of the representatives of faith communities is to be governed by the date of their assumption in their present office, their representatives being given the same relative precedence.

[9] This precedence to be given to the Chief of the Defence Staff and the Commissioner of the Royal Canadian Mounted Police on occasions when they have official functions to perform, otherwise they are to have equal precedence with Deputy Minis-

ters, with their relative position to be determined according to the respective dates of their appointments to office. The relative precedence of Deputy Ministers and other high officials of the public service of Canada is to be determined from time to time by the Minister of Canadian Heritage in consultation with the Prime Minister.

The members of the Royal Family are not anywhere mentioned in the promulgated Table of Precedence for Canada nor were they mentioned in the earliest versions of the table discussed previously. Their absence from the table reflects the fact that the Sovereign and other members of the Royal Family are not residents of this country, except for brief sojourns on state or private visits.[3] However, it is considered that the members of the Royal Family take precedence immediately after the Governor General, or Administrator of Canada, as the Governor General or Administrator is the constitutional representative of the Sovereign in Canada. This principle is acknowledged by the Canadian Armed Forces which provides the following guidance for applying the Table of Precedence for Canada in circumstances where members of the Royal Family are present: "Members of the Royal Family, other than Her Majesty The Queen[4] when in Canada, take precedence after the Governor-General."[5]

Normally, a royal visit to Canada will involve only a member of the Royal Family together with their consort. Therefore, precedence within the Royal Family will not be an issue concerning any state ceremony or formal occasion. Should multiple members of the Royal Family be present, however, reference can be

3. H.M. King Edward VIII did own a ranch in Alberta for some time but it was never established as a royal residence.

4. Now His Majesty the King, since the accession of King Charles III on September 8, 2022.

5. *The Heritage Structure of the Canadian Forces Chapter 1 – Precedence, Section 1, Order of Precedence for Individuals,* issued under the authority of the Chief of the Defence Staff, April 1, 1999, Department of National Defence, Ottawa, 1999.

made to the Table of Precedence for the members of the Royal Family in the United Kingdom.

In comparing the current Table of Precedence for Canada to the original Table of Precedence for Canada approved by Queen Victoria after confederation the most prominent change from the original is the elevation of federal government notables to the highest positions in the table. The Prime Minister is now recognized and placed high in the precedential order following the Governor General and the Prime Minister is followed by the Chief Justice of Canada and the parliamentary speakers. Even the members of the Privy Council forming the Canadian Ministry and the Leader of the Opposition in Parliament now rank above the Lieutenant Governors of the provinces who represent the King in each province. However, this table is slightly deceiving because the accompanying notes that form part of the table provide for the precedence of other individuals in certain circumstances. To obtain a true understanding of the national order of precedence in Canada it is necessary to incorporate the precedence granted by the notes and the actual text of the Table of Precedence which I have done below.

An Expanded Table of Precedence for Canada

To obtain a true understanding of the precedence established by the national Crown it is necessary to expand the official table by incorporating the precedence granted by the notes to the Table of Precedence of the Department of Canadian Heritage and applying the interpretation provided by the Department of National Defence for those occasions when members of the Royal Family are present. What follows is an expanded version of the Table of Precedence that takes into account these considerations.

An Expanded Table of Precedence for Canada

1. THE SOVEREIGN

34

2. The Governor General of Canada or the Administrator of the Government of Canada[6][7]

3. Members of the Royal Family other than the Sovereign in their Order of Precedence within the Royal Family.[8]

4. The Prime Minister of Canada

5. The Chief Justice of Canada

6. Former Governors General ranked by the date that they left office (most senior date first).

7. Widows and Widowers of deceased former Governors General ranked by the date that the deceased Governor General left office (most senior date first)[9]

8. Former Prime Ministers of Canada ranked by the date that they first became Prime Ministers of Canada.

9. Former Chief Justices of Canada ranked by the date of their appointment as Chief Justice of Canada (most senior date first).

10. The Speaker of the Senate

11. The Speaker of the House of Commons

---

6. The Administrator of Canada presides over the Government of Canada when the Governor General is absent from Canada, incapacitated or the office of Governor General is vacant. The Chief Justice of Canada is permanently designated to fulfill the role of Administrator but if the Chief Justice is unavailable the most senior remaining puisne Justice of the Supreme Court is designated to be the Administrator.

7. In the absence of the Governor General precedence is given to the Lieutenant Governor of the province, if present for the occasion or ceremony.

8. *The Heritage Structure of the Canadian Forces,* Issued on Authority of the Chief of the Defence Staff, Department of National Defence, Ottawa, 1999, Chapter 1-Precedence, Section 1 - Order of Precedence for Individuals, para. 5.

9. This does not apply where the spouse was not the spouse of the Governor General during the Governor General's term of office.

12. Ambassadors and High Commissioners, ranked *pari passu* by the date of presentation of their credentials to the Governor General[10]

13. Ministers Plenipotentiary[11]

14. Chargés d'Affaires[12]

15. Members of the Canadian Ministry being Members of the Cabinet ranked by the date of their appointment to the King's Privy Council for Canada.

16. Members of the Canadian Ministry being Ministers of State ranked by the date of their appointment to the King's Privy Council for Canada[13]

17. The Leader of the Opposition unless the incumbent is a former Prime Minister in which case see number 8 above.

18. The Lieutenant Governor of Ontario

19. The Lieutenant Governor of Quebec

20. The Lieutenant Governor of Nova Scotia

---

10. Ambassadors are diplomats accredited to a sovereign while High Commissioners are accredited to governments. Commonwealth countries exchange High Commissioners rather than ambassadors but both types of diplomat are considered to be equal by the Government of Canada.

11. A Minister Plenipotentiary is a diplomat ranking below an ambassador but having full powers to deal with the government to which he or she has been accredited.

12. A Chargés d'Affaires is a lower-ranking diplomat who represents his country to the country to which he or she is accredited while the accredited ambassador is absent or the office is vacant. If more than one is present they will be ranked by the relative precedence of their ambassadors.

13. All persons sworn into office as a Minister or Minister of State are members of the Canadian Ministry but admission to the Cabinet is by invitation of the Prime Minister. Ministers of State generally hold minor responsibilities and may be excluded from membership in the Cabinet, although that is not always the case.

21. The Lieutenant Governor of New Brunswick

22. The Lieutenant Governor of Manitoba

23. The Lieutenant Governor of British Columbia

24. The Lieutenant Governor of Prince Edward Island

25. The Lieutenant Governor of Saskatchewan

26. The Lieutenant Governor of Alberta

27. The Lieutenant Governor of Newfoundland and Labrador[14]

28. Members of the King's Privy Council for Canada, not of the Canadian Ministry, in accordance with the date of their appointment to the Privy Council but with precedence given to those who bear the honourary title "Right Honourable" in accordance with the date of receiving that honourary title.[15]

29. Premiers of the Provinces of Canada in the same order as Lieutenant Governors where the occasion or ceremony is federal.[16]

30. The Commissioner of the Northwest Territories[17]

31. The Commissioner of the Yukon Territory[18]

---

14. The rankings of provincial Lieutenant Governors are in the order in which their provinces joined the confederation. The precedence afforded to Lieutenant Governors in this national Table of Precedence applies where the occasion or ceremony is primarily federal. Where the occasion or ceremony is provincial, provincial orders of precedence will apply.

15. Generally the title of *Right Honourable* is given only to the Governors General, the Prime Minister, and the Chief Justice of Canada and is held for life.

16. Where the occasion or ceremony is provincial, provincial orders of precedence will apply.

17. Where the occasion or ceremony is territorial, territorial orders of precedence will apply.

18. Where the occasion or ceremony is territorial, territorial orders of precedence will apply.

32. The Commissioner of Nunavut where the occasion or ceremony is federal.[19]

33. Premiers of the Territories of Canada in the same order as Commissioners where the occasion or ceremony is federal.[20]

34. Representatives of faith communities being senior Canadian representatives of faith communities having a significant presence in a relevant jurisdiction ranking *pari passu*. The relative precedence of the representatives of faith communities is to be governed by the date of their assumption in their present office.

35. Puisne Judges of the Supreme Court of Canada

36. The Chief Justice and the Associate Chief Justice of the Federal Court of Canada

37. Chief Justices of the highest court of each Province and Territory with precedence governed by the date of appointment as Chief Justice.

38. Chief Justices and Associate Chief Justices of the other superior courts of the Provinces and Territories with precedence governed by the date of appointment as Chief Justice.

39. Judges of the Federal Court of Canada with precedence governed by the date of their judicial appointment.

40. Puisne Judges of the superior courts of the Provinces and Territories with precedence governed by the date of their judicial appointment.

41. Chief Judge of the Tax Court of Canada

---

19. Where the occasion or ceremony is territorial, territorial orders of precedence will apply.
20. Where the occasion or ceremony is provincial, provincial orders of precedence will apply.

42. Associate Chief Judge of the Tax Court of Canada

43. Judges of the Tax Court of Canada with precedence governed by the date of their judicial appointment.

44. Senators of Canada

45. Members of the House of Commons

46. Consuls General of countries without diplomatic representation.[21]

47. Clerk of the Privy Council and Secretary to Cabinet[22]

48. The Chief of the Defence Staff and the Commissioner of the Royal Canadian Mounted Police.[23]

49. Speakers of Legislative Assemblies, within their Province and Territory

50. Members of Executive Councils, within their Province and Territory

51. Judges of Provincial and Territorial Courts, within their Province and Territory

21. A country may not have an embassy or high commission in Canada nor an accredited ambassador or high commissioner but may have appointed a Consul General, Consul, or honourary Consul to deal with minor matters mostly involving trade, investment, and issues concerning the citizens of the country of the Consul while those citizens are within Canadian jurisdiction.

22. The Clerk of the Privy Council and Secretary to the Cabinet is the most senior permanent civil servant in the Canadian Government. He or she is regarded as the Head of the Public Service of Canada.

23. This precedence is granted to the Chief of the Defence Staff and the Commissioner of the Royal Canadian Mounted Police on occasions when they have official functions to perform, otherwise their precedence, if any, is equal to that of Deputy Ministers with whom they rank *pari passu* and is in the gift of the Minister of Canadian Heritage in consultation with the Prime Minister.

52. Members of Legislative Assemblies, within their Province and Territory

53. Chairperson of the Canadian Association of Former Parlia-mentarians[24]

Although, for protocol at ceremonial events the spouses of the individuals named in the Table of Precedence are not given any official precedence they will nevertheless be accorded the same precedence as their officially recognized husband or wife. In certain cases, as, for instance, where a spouse is representing an absent husband or wife who appears in the Table of Precedence the spouse may be accorded the appropriate precedence in their stead.

24. An association of former politicians.

CHAPTER 7.

PROVINCIAL TABLES OF PRECEDENCE

After confederation in 1867, some confusion reigned over the role of the Crown at the federal (then called Dominion) level and the role of the Crown at the provincial level. Originally, the founders of the new state of Canada in 1867 thought that the federal government was paramount and that the provinces were essentially a subordinate level of government. However, that view underwent considerable change when the courts began to interpret the *British North America Act*[1] (Now the *Constitution Act, 1867.*[2]). The courts began to assert the theory that the Crown in right of Canada (i.e. the federal part of the Crown) and the Crown in right of the provinces (the provincial component of the Crown) were indivisible and therefore equal. In *Lenoir v Ritchie,* [1879] 3 SCR 575 (Canada, S.C.C.) the Supreme Court held that while the Crown in right of Canada held constitutional jurisdiction to create dignities and honours as an aspect of the royal prerogative, the provinces could also create provincial dignities and honours by statute, thus empowering the Crown in right of a province to also make such awards. In that way, the court acknowledged a parity between the two aspects of the Crown in the new federal state.

In *The Queen v The Bank of Nova Scotia,* [1885] 11 SCR 1 (Canada S.C.C.) the Supreme Court of Canada found that the Crown in right of Canada could assert a priority in the recovery of a debt as part of the royal prerogative in as full a measure as could

---

1. 30 & 31 Victoria, c. 3 (UK)

2. RSC 1985, Appendix II, No. 5 . The title was amended by the *Canada Act 1982, c. 11 (U.K.).*

the Crown in right of a province on the basis that the Crown was indivisible as between the federal and provincial governments. That case established the equality of the Crown in right of Canada with the Crown in right of a province where a matter involved property and civil rights, a subject ordinarily within provincial jurisdiction.

That case was followed by an even more important judgment from the Judicial Committee of the Privy Council in London, England (which was then Canada's highest court) in *The Liquidators of the Maritime Bank of Canad v The Receiver-General of New Brunswick*, [1892] AC 437 (Canada P.C.) which answered the question of whether the Crown in right of a province possessed a like priority under the royal prerogative where there were debts owed to a province by an insolvent bank. In answering that question in the affirmative, the Imperial Privy Council held that "... a Lieutenant-Governor, [of a province] when appointed, is as much the representative of Her Majesty for all purpose of provincial government as the Governor-General himself is for all purposes of Dominion [i.e. federal] government".[3] As a result of these cases, it became clear that the indivisible Crown was equal in both its federal aspects and its provincial aspects.

The legal implication for the subject of precedence is that the Crown in the provinces and the Crown at the federal level of government are equal, although they exercise different jurisdictions, and that both the federal government and the provincial governments are therefore capable of exercising royal prerogative powers within their separate jurisdictions. Consequently, the provinces have also created tables of precedence to govern precedence within their provincial jurisdictions. Provincial tables of precedence will apply to ceremonies or proceedings at the provincial level of government to the exclusion of the rules of precedence prescribed by the Government of Canada.

3. At p. 443 of the judgment

The same result does not necessarily apply to the territorial governments because they are sub-sovereign entities and the Crown in the territories is the Crown in right of Canada. However, as a practical matter, the federal government may extend the same level of respect to territorial precedence as it does to provincial precedence.

Several provinces and territories (British Columbia, Alberta, Saskatchewan, Northwest Territories, Ontario, and Prince Edward Island) explicitly mention that where a particular ceremony involves federal, commonwealth, or international representatives, the federal Table of Precedence may be applied to the ceremony in lieu of the applicable provincial or territorial table.

In general, the provincial and territorial tables of precedence enjoy a great similarity but there are some distinctions between the various jurisdictions. Two provinces, Newfoundland and Labrador, and Saskatchewan, explicitly list the Sovereign in their tables, and Newfoundland and Labrador also places the Sovereign's consort into the table directly after the Sovereign. The other provinces and territories simply assume the Sovereign's place at the top of the order and begin their tables with his or her representative in the province, following the same practice as the federal Table of Precedence. Most provinces and territories also create placements for the leaders of aboriginal first nations within their provinces and several recognize Ambassadors and High Commissioners posted to Canada by foreign states (and New Brunswick also specifically recognizes Ministers Plenipotentiary and Chargés d'affaires appointed to Canada). In two provinces, New Brunswick and Quebec, the Speaker (or President) of the legislative assembly is given a high placement within the provincial order of precedence. Quebec places the President of the National Assembly in the 3rd place and the Speaker of the New Brunswick Legislative Assembly is placed fourth in the New Brunswick table. A few provinces have places provided for public officers who report directly to the Legislative Assembly, and some include the heads of Crown corporations. Most provinces and territories recognize senior officials of the provincial or territorial governments as well as mayors or senior local officials, while New Brunswick also includes municipal councillors. Uniquely, Newfoundland and Labrador recognizes persons who hold the Victoria Cross, the country's highest honour for military valour.

There are some precedential differences between the provinces and the territories. A territory is, in constitutional terms, a part of the country under the jurisdiction of the federal government although practically speaking they have evolved into pseudo-provinces that exercise many of the same powers and functions of a province through agreements with the federal government. Provincial status has hitherto eluded them, however, mainly due to the very small populations in the territories relative to the populations of most of the provinces. Unlike a province, where the Sovereign is represented by a Lieutenant Governor, the Crown's representative in the territories is actually the Governor General of Canada. Although many of the functions of a provincial Lieutenant Governor are performed within a territory by an official described as a Commissioner, that official represents the Minister of Northern Affairs in the federal cabinet, and not the Sovereign. The two territories that publish orders of precedence, Yukon and the Northwest Territories, have dealt with this difference in separate ways.

In the Yukon Table of Precedence, the Governor General of Canada is recognized first (and is immediately followed by the federal Prime Minister) and precedes the Commissioner of Yukon in the order of precedence. In the Northwest Territories, no mention is made of the Governor General (or the federal Prime Minister) and the order of precedence for the territory begins with the Commissioner of the Northwest Territories. Perhaps, the Northwest Territories merely assumes the precedence of the Governor General as the representative of the Sovereign within the territory in the same way that the federal government and most of the provinces simply assume the precedence of the Sovereign when implementing their tables of precedence.

The two northern territories also depart from the provincial tables in their orders of precedence in another way. Like several of the provinces, they grant precedence to members of the federal Senate and House of Commons. However, while the provinces that grant such precedence give priority to Senators above members of the House of Commons, the two territories have reversed that order and give precedence to members of the House of Commons above Senators. It would seem that the order of placement provided to Senators and members of the House of Commons by the provinces is preferable, as the Senate was meant to be the more august legislative body.

Below is a collection of the tables of precedence (official and unofficial) of the provinces and territories of Canada (note that the territory of Nunavut apparently does not have a published table of precedence).

PROVINCIAL TABLES OF PRECEDENCE

PROVINCE OF NEWFOUNDLAND AND LABRADOR[4]

Table of Precedence

1. The Sovereign (HM The King)
2. Consort of the Sovereign (HM The Queen)
3. Lieutenant Governor of Newfoundland and Labrador
4. Premier of Newfoundland and Labrador
5. Chief Justice of Newfoundland and Labrador
6. Speaker of the House of Assembly
7. Former Lieutenant Governors, in order of their departure from office
8. Former Premiers, in order of their departure from office

---

4. Unofficial table. Source: https://en.wikipedia.org/wiki/Order_of_precedence_in_Newfoundland_and_Labrador [accessed August 1, 2024]

9. Members of the Executive Council

10. Leader of the Opposition

11. Members of the King's Privy Council for Canada resident in Newfoundland and Labrador

12. Members of the Cabinet of Canada who represent Newfoundland and Labrador

13. Chief Justice of the Supreme Court of Newfoundland and Labrador

14. Associate Chief Justice of the Supreme Court of Newfoundland and Labrador

15. Puisne justices of the Court of Appeal

16. Justices of the Supreme Court of Newfoundland and Labrador

17. Chief Judge of the Provincial Court

18. Associate Chief Judge of the Provincial Court

19. Puisne judges of the Provincial Court

20. Associate Chief Judge of the Family Court

21. Puisne judges of the Family Court

22. Members of the House of Assembly (precedence governed by date of their first election to the Legislature)

23. Members of the Senate who represent Newfoundland and Labrador (precedence governed by date of appointment)

24. Members of the House of Commons who represent Newfoundland and Labrador (precedence governed by date of their first election to the House of Commons)

25. Roman Catholic Archbishop of St. John's

26. Bishop of Eastern Newfoundland & Labrador

27. Minister of the Presbyterian Church

28. Heads of Consular Post with jurisdiction in the Province of Newfoundland and Labrador (precedence governed by date of exequaturs)

29. Mayor of St. John's

30. Mayor of Corner Brook

31. Mayor of Mount Pearl

32. Mayors or other elected officials of incorporated municipalities (precedence governed alphabetically by municipality

name)

33. Recipients of the Victoria Cross resident in Newfoundland and Labrador

34. Commanding Officers (precedence governed by Canadian Armed Forces order of precedence: CFB Gander, CFB Goose Bay, CFS St. John's, HMCS Cabot

35. Chief of Police, Royal Newfoundland Constabulary

36. Commanding Officer "B" Division, Royal Canadian Mounted Police

37. High Sheriff of Newfoundland and Labrador

38. Members of the Order of Newfoundland and Labrador

39. Chancellor of Memorial University of Newfoundland

40. President and vice-chancellor of Memorial University of Newfoundland

PROVINCE OF PRINCE EDWARD ISLAND[5]

Order of Precedence:

1. The Lieutenant Governor, or in his or her absence from the Province, the Administrator.

2. The Premier.

3. The Mayor or other elected senior official of an incorporated municipality when the ceremony or event is hosted by or particularly involves that municipality.

4. The Chief Justice.

5. The Speaker of the Legislative Assembly.

6. Former Lieutenant Governors, with relative precedence governed by their date of leaving office.

7. Former Premiers, with relative precedence governed by their date of leaving office.

8. Members of the Executive Council.

9. The Chief Justice of the Supreme Court – Trial Division.

10. Justices of the Supreme Court of Prince Edward Island,

---

5. Source: https://www.princeedwardisland.ca/en/information/executive-council-office/table-of-precedence-for-prince-edward-island [accessed August 1, 2024]

with relative precedence governed by the date of appointment.

11. The Chief Judge of the Provincial Court.

12. Judges of the Provincial Court, with relative precedence governed by date of appointment.

13. Members of the Legislative Assembly (Leader of the Opposition, Leader of the Third Party, Deputy Speaker, Government House Leader, thereafter by date of first election, and if coincident, then alphabetically).

14. Members of the Senate (by date of appointment).

15. Members of Parliament (Members of the Federal Cabinet, then by date of first election, and if coincident, alphabetically).

16. Members of the Queen's [King's] Privy Council for Canada.

17. Chiefs of the Mi'kmaq First Nation.

18. Clerk of the Executive Council.

19. Mayors or other elected senior officials of incorporated municipalities, alphabetically by municipality name.

20. The Bishop of Charlottetown, the Bishop of Nova Scotia [and Prince Edward Island] and the President of the Queens County Ministerial Association, with relative precedence governed by date of appointment or election.

21. The Senior Officer of the Royal Canadian Mounted Police in Prince Edward Island.

22. The Presidents of the University of Prince Edward Island, Holland College and Collège d'Île.

23. Deputy Heads of Departments, Agencies, Commissions and Offices of the Provincial Government, with relative precedence governed by date of initial appointment as a Deputy Head.

Council approved a Table of Precedence for the Province of Prince Edward Island effective June 29, 2021. Further, Council rescinded Minute in Council No. 4/94 of July 14, 1994.

PROVINCE OF NOVA SCOTIA[6]

Table of Precedence

6. Source:https://novascotia.ca/iga/tableprec.asp [accessed August 1, 2024]

Published date: October 27, 2021

1. Lieutenant Governor of Nova Scotia
2. Premier of Nova Scotia
3. Chief Justice of Nova Scotia
4. Former Lieutenant Governors
5. Former Premiers
6. Speaker of the Nova Scotia House of Assembly
7. Members of the Executive Council of Nova Scotia
8. Leader of the Opposition
9. Members of the Queen's Privy Council for Canada resident in Nova Scotia
10. Member of the Federal Cabinet who represents Nova Scotia
11. Chief Justice of the Supreme Court of Nova Scotia
12. Associate Chief Justice of the Supreme Court of Nova Scotia
13. Associate Chief Justice of the Supreme Court of Nova Scotia (Family Division)
14. Justices of the Nova Scotia Court of Appeal
15. Justices of the Supreme Court of Nova Scotia
16. Chief Judge of the Provincial and Family Courts of Nova Scotia
17. Associate Chief Judge of the Provincial Court of Nova Scotia
18. Judges of the Provincial Court of Nova Scotia
19. Associate Chief Judge of the Family Court of Nova Scotia
20. Judges of the Family Court of Nova Scotia
21. Leader of the Third Party
22. Members of the Legislative Assembly of Nova Scotia (with precedence governed by the date of their first election to the Legislature)
23. Members of the Senate who represent Nova Scotia (with precedence governed by date of appointment)
24. Members of the House of Commons who represent Nova Scotia (with precedence governed by the date of their first election to the House of Commons)

25. Bishop of the Diocese of Nova Scotia and Prince Edward Island (Anglican)

26. Archdiocese of Halifax-Yarmouth (Roman Catholic)

27. Leaders of Faith Communities

28. Consuls General[7]

29. Mayor of the Halifax Regional Municipality

30. Commander, Maritime Forces Atlantic and Joint Task Force Atlantic

31. Commander, 5th Canadian Division

32. Assistant Commissionaire, Royal Canadian Mounted Police

PROVINCE OF NEW BRUNSWICK[8]

Table of Precedence (Revised December 2023)

1. The Lieutenant Governor (see note 1)

2. The Premier

3. The Chief Justice of New Brunswick

4. The Speaker of the Legislative Assembly

5. Former Lieutenant Governors

6. Former Premiers

7. Former Chief Justices of New Brunswick

8. Ambassadors, High Commissioners, Ministers Plenipotentiary, and Chargés d'affaires with precedence to their date of appointment

9. Members of the Executive Council of New Brunswick with precedence in accordance with the Executive Council Act

10. Leader of the Opposition

11. Members of the Privy Council

12. Chief Justice of the Court of King's Bench

13. Associate Chief Justice of the Court of King's Bench

14. Members of the Senate

15. Members of the House of Commons

---

7. First the Consul General of France, and then the Consul General of the United States, are listed in the current version.

8. Source: https://www2.gnb.ca/content/gnb/en/departments/intergovernmental_affairs/protocol/precedence.html [accessed August 1, 2024]

16. Judges of the Court of Appeal with precedence according to their date of appointment

17. Judges of the Court of King's Bench with precedence according to their date of appointment

18. Members of the Legislative Assembly in the following order: Deputy Speaker, Government House Leader (see Note 2), Opposition House Leader, Leaders of Unofficial Opposition Parties, other members with precedence according to their date and order of their swearing in as Members of the Legislature

19. Elders and Chiefs of New Brunswick Indigenous Peoples

20. Leaders of religious denominations with precedence according to their date of appointment or election to the present office

21. Chief Judge of the Provincial Court

22. Judges of the Provincial Court with precedence according to their date of appointment

23. Members of the Consular Corps in the following order: Consuls General, Consuls, Vice-Consuls, Honorary Consuls and Consular Agents with precedence among themselves according to their date of appointment

24. Mayors of the Cities of New Brunswick (with precedence given to the Mayor of the host municipality where appropriate) in the following order: Fredericton, Saint John, Moncton, Edmundston, Campbellton, Bathurst, Miramichi and Dieppe

25. Mayors of the Towns of New Brunswick with precedence among themselves according to the alphabetical order of the place-names

26. Mayors of the Villages, Rural Communities and Regional Municipalities of New Brunswick with precedence according to the alphabetical order of the place-names

27. Councillors of the Cities, Towns, Villages, Rural Communities and Regional Municipalities of New Brunswick in the same order of precedence among themselves according to the alphabetical order of their surnames

28. Clerk of the Legislative Assembly

29. Ombudsman

30. Child and Youth Advocate

31. Seniors' Advocate

32. Auditor General

33. Integrity Commissioner

34. Commissioner of Official Languages

35. Consumer Advocate for Insurance

36. Chief Electoral Officer

37. Clerk of the Executive Council

38. Deputy Heads of the Civil Service, with precedence according to their date of appointment

39. Heads of Crown Corporations and Agencies, with precedence according to their date of appointment

40. Commanding Officer of "J" Division, Royal Canadian Mounted Police

41. Commander of Canadian Forces Base Gagetown and Commander of the Combat Training Centre

42. Chancellors of New Brunswick Universities in the following order: University of New Brunswick, Mount Allison University, St. Thomas University and Université de Moncton

43. Presidents of the Universities of New Brunswick in the same order of precedence as the Chancellors

NOTES

1. In the absence of the Lieutenant Governor from the Province or his/her inability to carry out the duties of Lieutenant Governor for any reason, the Chief Justice becomes Administrator of the Province and takes the Lieutenant Governor's place of precedence.

2. A Government House Leader who is Cabinet Minister takes the precedence of a Cabinet Minister.

3. Members of the King's Privy Council for Canada who reside in New Brunswick take precedence after the Leader of the Opposition of New Brunswick. Members of the Privy Council who are members of the Cabinet take precedence over those who are not member of Cabinet by order of their appointment

to Cabinet. Other Privy Councillors take precedence by order of their appointment to the King's Privy Council of Canada.

PROVINCE OF QUEBEC[9]

**Ordre de préséance des autorités convoquées individu-
eliement dans les cérémonies publiques organisées par le
gouvernement du Québec**

1. Le lieutenant-gouverneur (A).
2. Le premier ministre (B)
3. Le président de lÀssemblée nationale
4. Le juge en chef du Québec
5. Le vice-premier ministre.
6. Les chefs de missions diplomatiques, suivis des dirigeants dòrganisations internationales gouvernementales ©
7. Les membres du Conseil des ministres (D)
8. Le chef de l"Opposition officielie, suivi des chefs des autres groupes dòpposition reconnus
9. Les vice-présidents de l`Assemblée nationale.
10. Le juge en chef de la Cour supérieure, suivi du juge en chef de la Cour du Québec (E).
11. Les chefs de postes consulaires, suivis des représentants au Québec d`États fédérés étrangers (F).
12. Le chef de l`Assemblée des Premiéres Nations du Québec et du Labrador et le président de la Société Makivik.
13. Le maire et le député de l`Assemblée nationale du lieu où se tient la cérémonie.
14. Le maire de la capitale nationale, le maire de la métropole, suivis des présidents des regroupements de municipalités (G).
15. Les députés de l`Assemblée nationale.
16. Le secrétaire général du Conseil exécutif et le secrétaire général de l`Assebleée nationale.
17. Les personnes désignées par l`Assemblée nationale.

9. Decree No: 1123-2019 dated May 2, 1990. Source:
   https://www.mrif.gouv.qc.ca/content/documents/fr/GUI-Ordre-preseance-
   autorites-gouvernement-quebec-MRIF.pdf [accessed August 1, 2024]

18. Les dirigeants des institutions d'enseignement universitaire et collégial.

19. Le chef de cabinet du premier ministre, les sous-ministres et le chef du Protocole.

20. Les principaux dirigeants des organismes gouvernementaux.

21. Les juges de la Cour d'appel, suivi des juges de la Cour supérieure et des juges de la Cour du Québec.

22. Les anciens députés de l'Assemblée nationale (H).

23. Le président de l'Ordre national du Québec, suivi des membres de l'Ordre en fonction de leur grade.

Notes

A. Les anciens lieutenant-gouverneurs du Québec, selon la date de cessation de leurs fonctions, prennent place après le juge en chef du Québec.

B. Les premiers ministres ayant précédé le premier ministre en fonction le suivent, selon la date de cessation de leurs fonctions.

C. La préséance des chefs de missions diplomatiques entre eux est accordée au doyen du corps diplomatique, suivi des autres chefs de missions diplomatiques.

D. La préséance des ministres entre eux est déterminée par le premier ministre lis sont immédiatement suivis par leurs homologues fédéraux.

E. Les juges en chef de la Cour supérieure et de la Cour du Québec sont suivis des juges en chef accociés et des juges en chef adjoints de ces cours.

F. La préséance des chefs de postes consulaires entre eux est accordée au doyen du corps consulaire, suivi des chefs de poste ayant résidence à Québec et des autres chefs de postes ayant résidence ailleurs au Québec.

G. Aprés le maire de Québec, capitale nationale, et celui de Montréal, métropole, suivent les présidents des deux regroupements municipaux que sont 'Union des municipalités du Québec et la Fédération québécoise des municipalités locales et régionales (FQM) ainsi que les maires des grandes villes du

Québec (comptant plus de 100 000 habitants) que sont Laval, Gatineau, Longueuil, Sherbrooke, Saguenay, Lévis, Trois-Riviéres et Terrebonne. Les maires des autres municipalités viennent ensuite par ordre alphabétique du nom de la municipalité. H. Les ancients présidents de l`Assemblée nationale sont également reconnus au titre dàncients députés.

PROVINCE OF ONTARIO[10]

Ontario Order of Precedence

1. Lieutenant governor of Ontario or the Administrator
2. Premier of Ontario
3. Chief Justice of Ontario
4. Former lieutenant governors of Ontario, with relative precedence among them governed by the date of their leaving office
5. Former premiers of Ontario, with relative precedence among them governed by the dates of their first assumption of office
6. Speaker of the Legislative Assembly of Ontario
7. Heads of accredited diplomatic missions in Ottawa with relative precedence to be determined by the date they present their credentials to the Governor General of Canada
8. Members of the Executive Council of Ontario, in accordance with the precedence document issued by the Cabinet Office
9. Leader of the Official Opposition
10. Members of the Privy Council for Canada resident in Ontario
11. Chief Justice of the Superior Court of Justice
12. Associate Chief Justice of Ontario
13. Associate Chief Justice of the Superior Court of Justice
14. Chief Justice and the Associate Chief Justices of the Ontario Court of Justice
15. Judges of the Ontario Court of Appeal
16. Judges of the Superior Court of Justice
17. Members of the Legislative Assembly of Ontario with

10. Source: https://www.ontario.ca/page/order-precedence#section-1 [accessed August 1, 2024]

precedence governed by the date of their first election to the Legislature

18. Either: [a] Members of the Senate who represent Ontario with relative precedence among them determined by the date of appointment [or] [b] Members of the House of Commons who represent Ontario constituencies with relative precedence among them determined by the date of election, and alphabetically for those elected at the same election

19. Heads of religious denominations

20. Heads of consular post with jurisdiction in the Province of Ontario with precedence governed by date of exequatur

21. Judges of the Ontario Court of Justice

22. Either: [a] Chair of the host regional municipality (where applicable) [or] [b] Host mayor

23. Either: [a] Other chairs of regional municipalities (where applicable) [or] [b] Other mayors with relative precedence governed by the date of appointment or election to office

24. Indigenous leaders: Chiefs of First Nations in Ontario

25. Either: [a] Deputy ministers, with precedence governed by date of appointment [or] [b] Other Ontario Public Service officials with the rank and status of deputy ministers, with precedence governed by date of appointment

PROVINCE OF MANITOBA[11]

Order of Precedence for Manitoba

1. The Lieutenant-Governor of Manitoba

2. The President of the Executive Council of Manitoba (otherwise known as the Premier of Manitoba)

3. The Chief Justice of Manitoba

4. Former Lieutenant Governors of Manitoba or surviving spouses in order of seniority in taking office

5. Former Presidents of the Executive Council of Manitoba in order of seniority in taking office

11. Source: https://www.gov.mb.ca/fpir/protocol/precedence.html [accessed August 1, 2024]

6. Members of the Privy Council of Canada resident in Manitoba by order of seniority of taking the Oath of Office

7. Members of the Executive Council of the Province of Manitoba in relative order of seniority of appointment

8. The Chief Justice of the Court of Queen's Bench

9. The Speaker of the Legislative Assembly of Manitoba

10. The Puisne Judges of the Court of Appeal and of the Court of Queen's Bench in relative order of seniority of appointment

11. The Leader of the Official Opposition in the Legislative Assembly of Manitoba

12. The Archbishop of St. Boniface

13. The Bishop of Rupert's Land

14. The Archbishop of Winnipeg

15. The Metropolitan of the Ukrainian Orthodox Church

16. The Metropolitan of the Ukrainian Catholic Church

17. The President of the Manitoba Conference of the United Church of Canada

18. The Chair of the Manitoba Conference of the Presbyterian Church in Canada

19. The Chair of other representatives persons of the following denominations as indicated below and whose person will be signified to the Clerk of the Executive Council from time to time: Lutheran Church; Jewish Rabbi; The Mennonite Faith; The Baptist Church; The Salvation Army; The Pastors Evangelical Fellowship

20. Members of the House of Commons resident in Manitoba by order of seniority in taking office

21. Members of the Legislative Assembly of Manitoba in relative order of seniority in taking office

22. Provincial Court Judges in relative order of seniority of appointment

23. Magistrates in relative order of seniority of appointment

24. Members of the local Consular Corps in relative order of seniority of appointment

25. Mayors, Reeves and elected local government administrators in relative order of date of taking office

PROVINCE OF SASKATCHEWAN[12]

Table of Precedence for Saskatchewan

The Chief of Protocol is responsible for interpretation of the following table:

His Majesty The King

1. The Lieutenant Governor of Saskatchewan or the Administrator. (see notes 2a and 2b)
2. The Premier of Saskatchewan. (see note 2b)
3. The Chief Justice of Saskatchewan. (see note 3)
4. The Speaker of the Legislative Assembly. (see note 2c)
5. The Deputy Premier, then Members of the Executive Council in relative order of precedence as determined by the Premier.
6. The Leader of the Opposition. (see note 2d)
7. The Chief Justice of the Court of King's Bench.
8. Superior Court Justices: Justices of the Court of Appeal and the Court of King's Bench, with relative precedence among them determined by date of first appointment to the Superior Courts.
9. Provincial Court: the Chief Judge, then the Associate Chief Judge(s), then Judges in order of seniority of appointment.
10. The Members of the Legislative Assembly, in the following order: Deputy Speaker; the Government House Leader (see note 4); the Opposition House Leader; the other Members, with relative precedence to be determined by date of first election to the Legislature. (see note 2e)
11. Indigenous Leaders: Elders, the Chief and Vice-Chiefs of the Federation of Sovereign Indigenous Nations (FSIN); the senior officers of the Tribal Councils; the Chiefs of Saskatchewan First Nation Bands; equivalent Métis leaders.
12. Leaders of Faith Communities: the Archbishop, or Senior

12. Source: https://www.saskatchewan.ca/government/visual-identity-and-protocol/protocol-guidelines/table-of-precedence [accessed August 1, 2024]

Bishop in the Province, of the Anglican Church of Canada; the Archbishop of Regina and Metropolitan, or the Senior Bishop in the Province, of the Roman Catholic Church; the Bishop of the Saskatoon Eparchy of the Ukrainian Catholic Church; the President, or the Past President or the President-Elect, of the Saskatchewan Conference of The United Church of Canada; the Bishop of the Saskatchewan Synod of the Evangelical Lutheran Church in Canada; the senior representatives in the Province of the Alliance, Baptist, Mennonite, Orthodox and Presbyterian Churches and of the Jewish, Muslim and Hindu Faiths. (Relative precedence among the various religious leaders is determined by the date of appointment or election to their present office.) (see note 6)

13. The Consular Corps in the Province, in the following order: Dean of the Consular Corps; Consuls-General; Consuls; Vice-Consuls; Consular Agents. (Relative precedence among them is determined by the date of their appointment.) (see note 6)

14. Mayors, with precedence given to the mayor of the host municipality and subsequent relative precedence determined by the date of first taking office. (see note 5)

15. Senior Officials:

a. the Deputy Minister to the Premier; the Cabinet Secretary and Clerk of the Executive Council; the Clerk of the Legislative Assembly; the seven officers of the Legislative Assembly including: the Ombudsman, the Provincial Auditor, the Chief Electoral Officer, the Advocate for Children and Youth, the Information and Privacy Commissioner, the Public Interest Disclosure Commissioner and the Conflict of Interest Commissioner. As well, the Human Rights Commissioner and the Treaty Commissioner.

b. Deputy Ministers; then other senior Saskatchewan government officials with rank of Deputy Minister as determined by the Executive Council; then Chief Executive Officers of Crown Corporations – relative precedence determined by date of appointment (see note 6).

16. Universities: the Chancellor of the University of

Saskatchewan; the Chancellor of the University of Regina; the President of the University of Saskatchewan; the President of the University of Regina, and the President of the First Nations University of Canada.

17. Police and Military: the Commanding Officer of "F" Division, Royal Canadian Mounted Police; the Commanding Officer of "Depot" Division, Royal Canadian Mounted Police; the President of the Saskatchewan Association of Chiefs of Police; the Wing Commander of 15 Wing Moose Jaw; the senior representative in Saskatchewan of 38 Canadian Brigade Group; the senior representative in Saskatchewan of Maritime Command.

Explanatory Notes

1. The above Table of Precedence is intended for provincial occasions.

2. On federal-provincial occasions, or on occasions when federal, diplomatic, foreign or Commonwealth representatives are present, the Table of Precedence for Canada, international protocol rules, and other courtesies may alter the Saskatchewan order. Specific cases are as follows:

A. His Majesty The King has precedence over everyone. Other members of the Royal Family have precedence immediately after the Lieutenant Governor.

B. When present on provincial occasions the Governor General and the Prime Minister take precedence after the Lieutenant Governor and the Premier respectively. They may, as a courtesy and at the discretion of the Province, be granted precedence over the Lieutenant Governor and the Premier respectively on federal-provincial occasions taking place within the province.

C. Heads of diplomatic missions accredited to Canada (Embassies and High Commissions) may be given precedence immediately after the Speaker of the Legislative Assembly, with seniority as determined by Foreign Affairs Canada.

D. Precedence may be given immediately after the Leader of the Opposition to Members of the King's Privy Council for

Canada, first to members of the Canadian Cabinet, then to Privy Councillors who are not members of the Cabinet, in each case relative precedence to be in order of the date of appointment.

E. Precedence may be given immediately after the Members of the Legislative Assembly of Saskatchewan to:

I. Members of the Senate who represent Saskatchewan, relative precedence determined by date of appointment;

II. Members of the House of Commons who represent Saskatchewan constituencies, relative precedence determined by date of election.

3. Precedence is given immediately after the Chief Justice of Saskatchewan to former Lieutenant Governors, then former Premiers, then former Chief Justices of Saskatchewan; relative precedence in each sub-category to be determined by date of first appointment to office. (Former Premiers who continue to hold other elected office are accorded the precedence attached to that office.)

4. A Government House Leader who is a Cabinet Minister takes the precedence of a Cabinet Minister.

5. On municipal occasions, the Mayor or other senior elected official of the municipality has precedence immediately after the Premier.

6. When a number of persons were elected or appointed to office on the same date, precedence shall be determined by alphabetical order of their last names.

PROVINCE OF ALBERTA[13]

Order of Precedence

1. The Lieutenant Governor of Alberta*
2. The Premier of Alberta.
3. The Chief Justice of Alberta
4. Former Lieutenant Governors, precedence determined by

13. Source: https://www.alberta.ca/protocol-order-of-precedence#jumplinks-0 [accessed August 1, 2024]

the date of their Commissions

5. Former Premiers; precedence is determined by the date of their swearing-in ceremony

6. The Speaker of the Legislative Assembly of Alberta

7. Ambassadors and High Commissioners accredited to Canada

8. Members of the Executive Council of Alberta, in relative order of precedence as determined by the Premier

9. Leader of the Official Opposition

10. Members of the Privy Council for Canada resident in Alberta, with relative precedence among them to, first, Members of the Canadian Cabinet and second, to those not in Cabinet

11. Members of the Legislative Assembly of Alberta with precedence governed by the date of their first election to the Legislature

12. Members of the Senate, who represent Alberta, relative precedence determined by date of appointment

13. Members of the House of Commons who represent Alberta constituencies, relative precedence determined by date of election

14. Chief Justice, Alberta Court of King's Bench

15. Justices of the Alberta Court of Appeal

16. Justices of the Alberta Court of King's Bench

17. Heads of religious denominations

18. Heads of Consular Posts: Consuls-General; Consuls; Vice-Consuls; Consular Agents. (Precedence is determined by the date that definitive recognition is given by the Governor General.)

19. Chief Judge of the Court of Justice followed by judges in seniority of appointment

20. Mayors

21. Aboriginal Leaders: Chiefs of the Treaty First Nations in Alberta, in order of seniority of election to office; President of Metis Settlements General Council; President of Métis Nation of Alberta

22. Senior Officials:

A. The Deputy Minister to the Premier and Cabinet Secretary; the Clerk of the Legislative Assembly; the Ombudsman; the Provincial Auditor; the Chief Electoral Officer; the Ethics Commissioner, the Information and Privacy Commissioner, the Child and Youth Advocate, and the Public Interest Commissioner

B. Deputy Ministers; then Senior Alberta government officials with rank of Deputy Minister as determined by the Executive Council; then Chief Executive Officers of Crown Corporations (relative precedence determined by date of appointment)

C. Universities: The Chancellor of the University of Alberta; Chancellor of the University of Calgary; Chancellor of the University of Lethbridge; Chairman of the Board, University of Alberta; Chairman of the Board, University of Calgary; Chairman of the Board, University of Lethbridge; Chairman of the Board, Athabasca University; Chairman of the Board, Mount Royal University; Chairman of the Board, Grant MacEwan University; President of the University of Alberta; President of the University of Calgary; President of the University of Lethbridge; President of Athabasca University; President of Mount Royal University; President, Grant MacEwan University

D. Police and Military: Commanding Officer, "K" Division, Royal Canadian Mounted Police; Commander, 3rd Canadian Division; Commanding Officer, H.M.C.S. Nonsuch; Commanding Officer, 1 Canadian Mechanized Brigade Group; Commanding Officer, 1 Area Support Group; Commanding Officer, 41 Canadian Brigade Group; Commanding Officer, 4 Wing

*In the absence of the Lieutenant Governor from the Province or his/her inability to carry out the duties of Lieutenant Governor for any reason, the Administrator of the Province takes the Lieutenant Governor's place of precedence.

PROVINCE OF BRITISH COLUMBIA[14]

14. Unofficial. Source: https://web.archive.org/web/20130327133253/

Table of Precedence for British Columbia

1. The Lieutenant Governor of British Columbia([1] and [2])
2. The Premier of British Columbia[3]
3. The Chief Justice of British Columbia[4]
4. The Speaker of the Legislative Assembly of British Columbia
5. The Members of the Executive Council of British Columbia[5]
6. The Leader of the Official Opposition of British Columbia [6]
7. The Chief Justice of the Supreme Court of British Columbia
8. Church representatives of faith communities[7]
9. The Justices of the Court of Appeal of British Columbia with precedence to be governed by the date of appointment
10. The Puisne Justices of the Supreme Court of British Columbia with precedence to be governed by the date of appointment
11. The Judges of the County Courts of British Columbia with precedence to be governed by the date of appointment
12. The Members of the Legislative Assembly of British Columbia with precedence to be governed by the date of their first election to the legislature[8] (Subject to Note [6])
13. The Chief Judge of the Provincial Court of British Columbia
14. The Commander Maritime Forces Pacific
15. The Heads of Consular Posts with jurisdiction in British Columbia with precedence to be governed by Article 16 of the Vienna Convention on Consular Relations
16. The Mayor of Victoria
17. The Mayor of Vancouver
18. The Chancellors of the University of British Columbia, the University of Victoria and Simon Fraser University, respectively.

http://www.pch.gc.ca/pgm/ceem-cced/atc-ac/precbc-eng.cfm [accessed August 1, 2024]. Information provided by the Department of Canadian Heritage based on information received from the Protocol Office of British Columbia, December 1991.

NOTES

The Table of Precedence for British Columbia lists categories in their order of precedence as they apply to ceremonies and occasions of a provincial nature. At provincial functions where federal, foreign or diplomatic dignitaries are present, circumstances may dictate that provisions of the Table of Precedence of Canada or international rules of protocol be observed thus giving these dignitaries precedence over certain provincial categories. Similarly, circumstances may also dictate that precedence be given to host officials of lesser rank than dignitaries who may be present. When the date of appointment or election to office is the same, precedence within each category is determined by alphabetical order.

[1] In the absence of the Lieutenant Governor of British Columbia the Administrator of British Columbia assumes the role.

[2] Former Lieutenant Governors of British Columbia take precedence after the Chief Justice of British Columbia. Precedence among former Lieutenant Governors is governed by the date of their Commissions.

[3] Former Premiers of British Columbia take precedence after former Lieutenant Governors. Precedence among former Premiers is determined by the date of their accession to office.

[4] Subject to Notes 2 and 3, Heads of Accredited Diplomatic Missions in Ottawa take precedence after the Chief Justice of British Columbia.

[5] Members of the Executive Council take precedence from the Ministry for which they are responsible. Precedence of Ministries in British Columbia is determined by the date of origin of the Ministry.

[6] Members of the Queen's Privy Council for Canada who reside in British Columbia take precedence after the Leader of the Official Opposition of British Columbia. Privy Councillors who are members of the Cabinet take precedence over those who are not members of the Cabinet by order of their

first appointment to the Cabinet. Other Privy Councillors take precedence by order of their appointment to the Queen's Privy Council for Canada.

[7] Precedence among ecclesiastical dignitaries is to be governed by the date of their accession to their present office.

[8] Members of the Legislative Assembly of British Columbia are followed in precedence by:

Members of the Senate who represent British Columbia by order of their appointments; and

Members of the House of Commons who represent British Columbia ridings by order of their first election to the House of Commons.

TERRITORY OF YUKON[15]

Order of Precedence

1. Governor General of Canada
2. Prime Minister of Canada
3. Commissioner of Yukon
4. Premier of the Yukon
5. federal Cabinet members
6. Speaker of the Yukon Legislative Assembly
7. Yukon First Nations Chiefs
8. Grand Chief of the Executive of the Council of Yukon First Nations
9. Ambassador or High Commissioner (Foreign) accredited to Canada
10. Justice of the Supreme Court of Yukon
11. Members of the Government of Yukon Executive Council (Cabinet)
12. Leader of the Official Opposition
13. Members of the Yukon Legislative Assembly
14. Member of Parliament for Yukon
15. Member of the Senate for Yukon
16. RCMP Divisional Commander

15. Source: https://yukon.ca/en/order-precedence [accessed August 1, 2024]

17. Armed Forces Commander

18. Judge or Justice of the Territorial Court

19. Heads of Consular Posts (Foreign)

20. Mayors

21. Government of Yukon deputy ministers and senior officials with the status of deputy ministers

22. presidents or executive directors of non-governmental organizations

23. Courtesy: Other dignified positions (such as former Commissioners or government leaders, current councillors, Elders)

NORTHWEST TERRITORIES[16]

Table of Precedence

A Table of Precedence identifies the order in which dignitaries are to be recognized/seated/addressed at official functions. Tables of Precedence reflect the importance of the position held by an individual. The order of precedence is determined first by rank and then by the length of service. Most provinces and territories have adopted their own Tables of Precedence. Listed below is the Table of Precedence for the Northwest Territories.

1. The Commissioner of the NWT or the Deputy Commissioner in her/his absence

2. The Premier of the NWT

3. Regional Aboriginal Leaders, with host region being first and other leaders' precedence determined by date of election

4. The Chief Justice of the Court of Appeal of the NWT and/or other members of the Court of Appeals who are not resident members of the Supreme Court

5. The Speaker of the Legislative Assembly of the Northwest Territories

6. Members of the Executive Council of the Northwest Territo-

---

16. Source: https://www.eia.gov.nt.ca/en/table-precedence [accessed August 1, 2024]

ries
7. The Senior Justice and/or Justices of the Supreme Court in the NWT
8. Members of the Legislative Assembly of the NWT, with precedence governed by the date of their first election to the Legislature
9. Federal Member of Parliament for the NWT
10. Member of the Senate from the NWT
11. The Chief Judge of the Territorial Court of the NWT
12. National Chief of the Dene Nation
13. Band Chiefs / Inuvialuit Community Corporation Presidents / Métis Presidents / Mayors, with host community being first and other chiefs/presidents/mayors' precedence determined by date of election.
14. RCMP Divisional Commander
15. Armed Forces Commander

The Table of Precedence for the NWT lists categories in their order of precedence as they apply to ceremonies and occasions of a territorial nature. At territorial functions where federal, foreign or diplomatic dignitaries are present, circumstances may dictate that the Table of Precedence of Canada or international rules of protocol be observed, thus giving these dignitaries precedence over certain territorial categories. Similarly, circumstances may also dictate that precedence be given to host officials of lesser rank than dignitaries who may be present. When the date of appointment or election to office is the same, precedence within each category is determined by alphabetical order.

• Former Commissioners of the NWT take precedence immediately after the Chief Justice of the Court of Appeal of the NWT. Precedence among former Commissioners is in order of seniority of taking Office.
• Former Government Leaders or Premiers of the NWT take precedence after former Commissioners of the NWT. Precedence among former government leaders and premiers are in

order of seniority in taking Office.

• Members of the Federal Cabinet and Privy Councilors not of the Cabinet would be given precedence immediately after the Premier, when in attendance at territorial functions.

• Deputy Judges or Justices from other jurisdictions would follow resident judges present.

CHAPTER 8.

SPECIAL FORMS OF PRECEDENCE IN CANADA

This chapter is concerned with the subject of specialized precedence concerning persons and groups of persons in the judicial, legal, and military professions.

Judicial Precedence

In Canadian courts precedence among judges is generally determined by the date of their appointment to the bench. However statutory rankings of precedence are sometimes seen as necessary in particular jurisdictions where there are separate trial and appeal courts, and where there is a desire to recognize the head of the trial court in relation to the head of the appeal court. In the provinces, for example, the head of the appeal court will normally bear the title of Chief Justice of the Province but the Chief Justice of the trial court will often be given precedence immediately after the Chief Justice of the Province and before the puisne judges of the appeal court, notwithstanding that an appeal court is higher in the judicial hierarchy than a trial court. There are several examples of this in Canada, which are set out in excerpts from the relevant legislation below.

Federal Courts of Canada Act[1]

6 (1) The Chief Justices of the Federal Court of Appeal and the Federal Court and the other judges of those courts have rank and precedence among themselves in the following order:

1. R.S.C., 1985, c. F-7 (as amended), s.6(1

(a) the Chief Justice of the Federal Court of Appeal;

(b) the Chief Justice of the Federal Court;

(b.1) the Associate Chief Justice of the Federal Court;

(c) the other judges of the Federal Court of Appeal, according to seniority determined by reference to the respective times when they became judges of the Federal Court of Canada or the Federal Court of Appeal; and

(d) the other judges of the Federal Court, according to seniority determined by reference to the respective times when they became judges of the Federal Court of Canada or the Federal Court.

Newfoundland and Labrador[2]

48. The judges of the Supreme Court and the Court of Appeal have rank, precedence and seniority in the following order:

(a) the Chief Justice of Newfoundland and Labrador ;

(b) the Chief Justice;

(c) the Associate Chief Justice;

(d) the judges of the Court of Appeal in the order of their seniority of appointment to the Court of Appeal; and

(e) the judges of the Supreme Court in the order of their seniority of appointment to the court. 1986 c42 s48; 2001 cN-3.1 s2; 2016 c37 s5; 2017 cC37.002 s46

Prince Edward Island[3]

2. Judicature Act, RSNL1990, C. J-4, s. 48, as am.

3. Judicature Act, SPEI, c. J-2.1, s. 24(1)

24. (1) The judges of the courts have rank and precedence as follows:

(a) the Chief Justice of Prince Edward Island;

(b) the Chief Justice of the Supreme Court;

(c) the other sitting judges of the Court of Appeal and the Supreme Court, according to
their seniority of appointment;

(d) the supernumerary judges, according to their seniority of appointment.

Nova Scotia[4]

22 (1) The Chief Justice of Nova Scotia shall have precedence over
all the other judges of the Court

(2) The Chief Justice of the Supreme Court shall have precedence
next after the Chief Justice of Nova Scotia over all other judges of the Court.

(3) The Associate Chief Justice of the Supreme Court shall have precedence next after the Chief Justice of the Supreme Court over all other judges
of the Court.

(3A) The Associate Chief Justice of the Supreme Court (Family Division) shall have precedence next after the Associate Chief Justice of the
Supreme Court over all other judges of the Court.

(4) The other judges of the Court of Appeal shall have precedence
next after the Associate Chief Justice of the Supreme Court

4. Judicature Act, R.S.N.S., c. 240, s. 22(1)

(Family Division)
according to seniority of appointment.

(5) The other judges of the Supreme Court shall have precedence
next after the judges of the Court of Appeal according to seniority of first appointment
to a court pursuant to section 96 of the Constitution Act, 1867.
R.S., c. 240, s. 22;
1992, c. 16, s. 49; 1997 (2nd Sess.), c. 5, s. 4.

Manitoba[5]

5. The Chief Justice of Manitoba has rank and precedence over all other judges of the courts of Manitoba, the Chief Justice of the Queen's Bench has rank and precedence next after the Chief Justice of Manitoba, and the other judges of the Court of Queen's Bench and of The Court of Appeal have rank and precedence among themselves according to their seniority of appointment.

British Columbia[6]

7 (1) The chief justice has rank and precedence over all other judges of the courts of British Columbia.

(2) The Chief Justice of the Supreme Court has rank and precedence over all other judges of the courts of British Columbia, other than the Chief Justice.

(3) The Associate Chief Justice of the Supreme Court has rank and precedence over all other judges of the courts of British Columbia, other than

(a) the chief justice, and

---

5. The Court of Appeal Act, R.S.M. 1987, c. C. 240, s. 5

6. Court of Appeal Act, SBC 2021, c. 6, s. 7.

(b) the Chief Justice of the Supreme Court.

(4) The justices holding office under section 3 (1) (b) and (2) have rank and precedence

(a) over all other judges of the courts of British Columbia other than

(i) the chief justice,

(ii) the Chief Justice of the Supreme Court, and

(iii) the Associate Chief Justice of the Supreme Court, and

(b) among themselves according to the seniority of their appointment to the court

Precedence at the Bar

In the mists of time, the Bar was the wooden railing in the courts of England at which a prisoner was arraigned or sentenced. Only the senior Barristers were permitted to be within the Bar, with junior counsel outside the Bar and therefore when a junior counsel was called to the Bar and invited to join senior counsel was a great honour for a young lawyer in the profession. But since at least the sixteenth century the Bar has become synonymous with the word "court" and to be called to the Bar is now to be admitted to practice as a lawyer before the courts of a province or territory.

Precedence at the Bar is concerned with the relative precedence of the lawyers who appear in a Canadian court in particular provinces or territories. Precedence, in this context, is largely a statutory precedence, and most provinces have enacted provisions to regulate the precedence of lawyers at the Bar. Although lawyers in Canada constitute an independent Bar, and the vast majority of lawyers are engaged in private practice, all lawyers in Canada are nevertheless deemed to be officers of the courts. As officers of the courts Canadian lawyers must maintain ethical standards of integrity, decorum, and an adherence to the rules of court whenever they have dealings with any of the courts of law. Independent associations of lawyers regulate the conduct of lawyers to ensure that they meet both their private obligations to their clients and their public obligations to the courts of law.

Lawyers in the Anglophone provinces and territories of Canada are called Barristers and Solicitors with the office of Barrister denoting an advocate in the higher courts, and the office of Solicitor describing lawyers who largely attend to the multifarious legal paperwork that is so essential to modern life, although some solicitors may appear on behalf of clients in the lower courts. However, unlike England, where there is a strict distinction between lawyers who are Barristers and those lawyers who are Solicitors, in Canada there is no rigid distinction and all lawyers in the Anglophone provinces are both Barristers and Solicitors and may therefore conduct any type of legal work.

In the province of Quebec, which follows the civil law tradition of France in private law matters, the organization of the legal profession is different. In Quebec, the legal profession is divided between l'avocat, or Advocates, who conduct proceedings on behalf of their clients in the courts of law, and le notaire or the Notary, who handles the legal work necessary to secure business and personal relationships, and to guard the value of transactions without conducting litigation in the courts. In this sense, the division of the legal profession in Quebec actually appears to be somewhat similar, at least superficially, to the organization of the legal profession in England.

Precedence has played an important role in the customs of Canadian courts, particularly on motion days when precedence has been used to determine which lawyers will be heard first on matters coming before the courts. In a crowded courtroom, the more senior lawyers will be heard first and then subsequently the more junior lawyers. The use of precedence has a two-fold advantage. Firstly, the time of senior lawyers is more valuable to their clients, and allowing them to quickly deal with their matters reduces the costs to their clients because lawyers' charges are based on seniority at the Bar and on billable hours. Secondly, allowing the senior lawyers to go first can provide instruction through observation to more junior lawyers, thus helping them to refine their skills in the courtroom.

The legal profession in Canada is regulated on a provincial basis and therefore each province has decided whether and how precedence will be recognized among Barristers and Solicitors appearing in the courts of a province. In general, precedence among Barristers and Solicitors is determined by the date that individual lawyers were admitted to the practice of law in the courts of a province. Where there has been a mass induction of new entrants to the profession the order of admission will be used to determine precedence.

There are several specific exceptions to this general rule concerning precedence at the Bar. However, these exceptions to the general rule of precedence are generally uncommon for the most part. Firstly, the law officers of the Crown, the Attorneys General of Canada and of the provinces, and the Solicitors General of Canada and the provinces, who represent the Crown in the courts of law have personal precedence in the courts, although such high officials rarely appear in person in court (and then only on the most significant cases). Additionally, most provinces also generally grant some precedence to lawyers who formerly held the offices of an Attorney General or Solicitor General for Canada or a province.

Secondly, following the precedence granted to former law officers of the Crown precedence is given in most provinces to a group of senior lawyers of marked distinction in the practice of law, who have been appointed to the office of King's Counsel (or Queen's Counsel if a woman occupies the throne). Such persons are appointed to this special office either by royal prerogative, in the case of the federal government, or pursuant to a statute enacted by a provincial government. Although they are formally described as "One of His Majesty's Counsel learned in the law" they are commonly known as King's Counsel and they can display the post-nominal abbreviation K.C. (or Q.C. if a Queen occupies the throne) after their name. A King's Counsel is given precedence at the Bar over the general mass of lawyers in a province and (generally) over any King's Counsel appointed after their appointment.

Finally, although rare, it is within the power of the federal government under the royal prerogative, or of the several provinces under statutory authority for the Crown to grant letters patent of precedence to an individual lawyer giving him or her precedence over other lawyers within that jurisdiction, according to the terms of their patent. At one time, in the nineteenth century, instances where the Crown granted patents of precedence were more common, as they were sought by some counsel in lieu of an appointment as a Queen's Counsel. The reasoning for seeking a patent of precedence in substitution for an appointment as a Queen's Counsel was due to the necessity for a Q.C. to obtain a licence from the Crown before commencing any action against the Crown on behalf of a private client. The delays and difficulties that once prevailed in obtaining such licences are no longer an issue for practising King's Counsel in Canada. The appointment of King's Counsel is now more tightly regulated than previously and as a result, the Crown at either level of government has generally been rather sparing in making such appointments.

The following tables illustrate the precedence of Barristers and Solicitors at the Bar of the Provinces and territories of Canada.

Precedence of Barristers and Solicitors in Newfoundland and Labrador[7]

7. *Queen's Counsel Act*, RSNL1990, c Q-2, as amended.

1. The Minister of Justice and Attorney General of Canada[8]
2. The Minister of Justice and Attorney General of Newfound-land and Labrador[9]
3. The Solicitor General of Canada[10]
4. Former Attorneys General of Canada and of Newfoundland and Labrador who are members of the Bar, ranked according to their seniority of appointment[11]
5. Former Solicitors General of Canada who are members of the Bar, ranked according to their seniority of appointment[12]
6. Queen's (King's) Counsel of Newfoundland and Labrador ranked according to the seniority of their appointment[13]
7. Members of the Bar ranked in the order of their admission to the Bar.[14]

Precedence of Barristers and Solicitors in New Brunswick[15]

1. Attorneys General of His Majesty[16]
2. King's Counsel or a person to whom a patent of precedence in the courts of New Brunswick has been granted by the Lieutenant Governor under the Great Seal of the Province[17]
3. The members of the Bar of New Brunswick in the order of their calls to the Bar of the Province.[18]

8. Ibid, s. 5(1)(a)

9. Ibid, s. 5(1)(b)

10. Ibid, s. 5(1)(c)

11. Ibid, s. 5(1)(d).

12. Ibid, s. 5(1)(e)

13. Ibid s. 5(1)(f)

14. Ibid, s. 5(1)(g)

15. *King's Counsel and Precedence Act*, SNB 2023, c.17, s.226

16. Ibid, s. 226(3), (6).

17. Ibid s. 226(4)(2)

18. Ibid s. 226 (5)

Precedence of Barristers and Solicitors in Prince Edward Island[19]

1. The Attorney General of Canada[20]
2. The Minister of Justice and Public Safety and Attorney General of Prince Edward Island[21]
3. Former Attorneys General of Canada and former Attorneys General of Prince Edward Island according to the seniority of their appointments[22]
4. King's Counsel according to the seniority of their appointments[23]
5. Members of the Prince Edward Island Bar in order of their admission[24]

Precedence of Barristers and Solicitors in Nova Scotia[25]

1. The Attorney General of Canada[26]
2. The Attorney General of Nova Scotia[27]
3. King's Counsel in Nova Scotia according to the seniority of their appointment[28]
4. Members of the Nova Scotia Bar in order of their call to the Bar.[29]

Precedence of l'avocats in Quebec[30]

---

19. *Legal Profession Act*, SPEI, c. L-6.1, s. 35
20. Ibid, s. 35(1)(a)
21. Ibid, s. 35(1)(b)
22. Ibid, s. 35(1)(c)
23. Ibid, s. 35(1)(d)
24. Ibid, s. 35(1)(e)
25. *Legal Profession Act*, SNS 2004, c. 28 s. 79
26. Ibid, s. 79(a)
27. Ibid, s. 79(b)
28. Ibid, s. 79(c)
29. Ibid, s. 79(d)
30. *Act respecting the Barreau du Québec*, S.Q. c. B-1, s. 11(2)

There is no established and maintained precedence for Advocates at the Bar of Quebec. There is a precedence granted to the Bâtonnier or head of the Quebec Bar so long as the former Bâtonnier remains a member of the Quebec Bar.

Precedence of Barristers and Solicitors in Ontario[31]

Precedence at the Bar of Ontario generally followed the practices in the other common law provinces of Canada until 2021. That year Ontario repealed provisions contained in the *Barristers Act* that governed precedence at the Bar of Ontario. Ontario took the step ostensibly to improve the efficiencies of the courts of law but also to respond to concerns expressed by members of the legal profession that the rule of precedence disadvantaged the members of the profession who are women, aboriginals, and racial minorities, and advantaged the older white male members of the profession.[32] The rule also excluded paralegals who are allowed to appear in a representative capacity in some of the lower courts and who are also regulated by the Law Society of Ontario, the same body that regulates lawyers in the province.[33]

In his remarks to the Ontario Legislature during debates on the repeal of the rule of precedence the Hon. Doug Downey, Attorney General of Ontario, stated that although precedence was being repealed, "The judge can order the hearings in the order that the judge wants. We're not constraining them. If they want

---

31. *Barristers Act*, RSO 1990, c. B.3, as amended by S.O. 2021, c. 34, Sched. 1

32. Melody Izadi, *Balance needed in deciding what order cases are handled*, May 29, 2019, Criminal Lawyers Toronto, https://cflaw.ca › blog › post › balance-needed-in-decid. [accessed July 31, 2024]; Glenn Kauth, *Dispute over paralegals sitting past bar before court today*, Canadian Lawyer (magazine), 01 Oct 201, https://www.canadianlawyermag.com/news/general/dispute-over-parale-gals-sitting-past-bar-before-court-today/271606 [accessed July 31,2024]

33. See the speech of the Attorney General of Ontario, Hon. Doug Downey regarding the *Supporting People and Businesses Act, 2021 / Loi de 2021 visant à soutenir la population et les entreprises*, Ontario Hansard, Session: 42-2, 2021-10-27

to make up their own rules and follow that, they can, but it's no longer going to be part of the law" suggesting that individual judges could follow precedence if that approach made sense to them, or they could implement other means of organization to promote efficiencies in the judicial process.

Precedence of Barristers and Solicitors in Manitoba[34]

1. The Attorney General of Canada[35]
2. The Solicitor General of Canada[36]
3. The Attorney General of Manitoba[37]
4. Lawyers who were formerly Attorneys General of Canada or Manitoba according to their seniority of appointment[38]
5. Lawyers who were formerly the Solicitor General of Canada according to their seniority of appointment[39]
6. King's Counsel appointed by the Governor General of Canada or by the Lieutenant Governor of any province according to their seniority of appointment[40]
7. Members of the Bar according to the seniority of their registration on the rolls of the law society[41]

Precedence of Barristers and Solicitors in Saskatchewan[42]

1. The Attorney General of Saskatchewan[43] [44]

---

34. *Legal Profession Act,* CCSM c. L 107, s. 84(1)

35. Ibid, s. 84(1)(a)

36. Ibid, s. 84(1)(b)

37. Ibid, s. 84(1)(c)

38. Ibid, s. 84(1)(d)

39. Ibid, s.84(1)(e)

40. Ibid, s. 84(1)(f)

41. Ibid, s. 84(1)(g)

42. *The King's Counsel Act* S.S. 2023, c. 29

43. Ibid, s. 4(a)

44. Although the precedence of the Attorney General of Canada is not specifically mentioned in section 4(a) of the Act, section 7(1) states that nothing in the act

2. Former Attorneys General of Canada or Saskatchewan who are members of the Bar of Saskatchewan ranked according to the seniority of their appointment as Attorney General[45]

3. Former Solicitors General of Canada who are members of the Bar of Saskatchewan ranked according to the seniority of their appointment as Solicitor General[46]

4. King's Counsel appointed by the Lieutenant Governor of Saskatchewan with precedence stipulated in their letters patent under the Great Seal of Saskatchewan[47]

5. The members of the Bar of Saskatchewan ranked according to the seniority of their enrollment.[48]

Precedence of Barristers and Solicitors in Alberta[49]

1. The Minister of Justice of Canada[50]
2. The Solicitor General of Canada[51]
3. The Minister of Justice of Alberta[52]
4. The Solicitor General of Alberta[53]
5. Former Ministers of Justice of Canada, Solicitors General of Canada, Attorneys General of Alberta, Ministers of Justice and Attorney General of Alberta, or Solicitors General of Alberta, ranked according to the seniority of their appointments[54]
6. King's Counsel of Alberta or members of the Bar of Alberta who have been granted a patent of precedence by the Lieu-

---

alters the rights of any Attorney General of His Majesty and subsection (2) preserves their right of precedence.

45. The King's Counsel Act S.S. 2023, c. 29, s. 4(b)

46. Ibid, s.4(c)

47. Ibid, s. 5

48. Ibid, s. 6

49. *King's Counsel Act*, RSA 2000, c. K-1, as am.

50. Ibid, s. 5(a)

51. Ibid, s. 5(b)

52. Ibid, s. 5(c)

53. Ibid, s. 5(c.1)

54. Ibid, s. 5(d)

tenant Governor under the Great Seal.[55]

7. Members of the Bar of Alberta ranked according to the order of their call to the Bar of Alberta.

Precedence of Barristers and Solicitors in British Columbia[56]

1. The Attorney General of Canada[57]
2. The Attorney General of British Columbia[58]
3. Former Attorneys General of Canada who served in office while being a member of the Bar of British Columbia and former Attorneys General of British Columbia ranked according to their seniority of appointment as Attorneys General[59]
4. Members of the Bar who formerly served as Solicitor General of Canada ranked according to their seniority of appointment as Solicitor General[60]
5. King's Counsel of British Columbia with relative precedence among King's Counsel being prescribed in their letters patent of appointment[61]
6. Members of the Bar ranked in the order of their call to the Bar.[62]

Precedence of Barristers and Solicitors in the Territories

There is no statutory precedence granted to Barristers and Solicitors in the northern territories of Yukon, Northwest Territories or Nunavut.

The Precedence of Military and Naval Formations in Canada

---

55. Ibid, s. 6

56. *King's Counsel Act* RSBC 1996, c. 393, a re-en and am.

57. Ibid, s. 6 (1)(a)

58. Ibid, s. 6(1)(b)

59. Ibid, s. 6 (1)(c)

60. Ibid, s. 6 (1)(d)

61. Ibid, s. 6 (1)(e), s. 6 (2), s. 6 (3

62. Ibid, s. 7

The Crown may exercise a royal prerogative power over the control of the armed forces of Canada though, for the most part, the organization and command of the armed forces are now largely regulated by statute.[63] Nevertheless, the powers of the royal prerogative over the armed forces remain extant. The Minister of National Defence retains overall authority and control of the armed forces on behalf of the Sovereign and his representative in Canada, the Governor General.

For protocol purposes, the precedence established for the various components of the armed forces is supported by the royal prerogative of the Crown concerning the control of the forces. Precedence has been reinforced by directives from the national defence command authority. The precedence of the Canadian armed forces stands as follows:

1. The Regular Force

a. Cadets of the Royal Military College of Canada and the College Militaire de St. Jean (parading as units)[64]
b. Headquarters personnel of the Department of National Defence
c. Royal Canadian Navy
d. Canadian Army
e. Royal Canadian Air Force
f. Canadian Joint Operations Command
g. Canadian Special Operations Forces Command
h. Military Personnel Command

2. The Reserve Force

a. Primary reserve
b. Supplementary reserve

---

63. Lordon, *Crown Law*, p. 81

64. Except when the Royal Canadian Horse Artillery parades with its guns. The RCHA then takes precedence.

c. Cadet Instructors cadre

d. Canadian Rangers

Within the armed forces as a whole the general principles of precedence follow the traditions inherited from Great Britain, with the navy being regarded as the senior service, followed by the army, and the air force as the most junior service. To this general principle exceptions have been made for military cadets parading together and for general staff headquarters to precede the three services. Specialized units drawing from all services are placed at the rear of the regular force.

Within the army, there is a precedential order established for the various active and reserve regiments. Generally, the precedential order followed is armoured units first (with horse guard regiments holding precedence within the armoured component) followed by the artillery (with horse artillery units taking precedence within the artillery component) followed by the combat engineering units, and finally the infantry. The specific precedence of individual units of the army is set out in an appendix.

Precedence of Medals and Decorations

There is an order of precedence for medals and decorations granted by the Crown in right of Canada and the Crown in right of a province that is established by the Governor General of Canada on the advice and recommendation of the King's Privy Council for Canada.[65] The subject of the precedence of medals and decorations is beyond the scope of this work, which is concerned with the precedence of persons either individually or in groups. For the current order of precedence for medals and decorations the Office of the Governor General of Canada may be consulted at (https://www.gg.ca/en/order-precedence).

---

65. The current instrument at the time of writing is Order in Council P.C. 1998-591, dated April 2, 1998.

CHAPTER 9.

DISPUTES OVER PRECEDENCE IN CANADA

Disputes involving precedence are relatively rare in modern times. Clear orders of precedence established by the Federal government and the governments of the provinces and territories have served to clarify the placements of high officials and others in the state. But disputes have nevertheless occurred and they have involved the highest official of the state resident in Canada, the Governor General.

Canada is a constitutional monarchy but it is a non-resident monarchy with the Sovereign of the United Kingdom serving in the capacity of King (or Queen) of Canada. Canada forms a part of a linked monarchy between the United Kingdom and some of Britain's former colonies which are collectively referred to as Commonwealth realms. The Sovereign is represented in Canada as a whole by the Governor General and is represented in each of the several provinces by Lieutenant Governors. It is a constitutional system of government that was established at confederation in 1867 and has prevailed since then, providing Canada with a system of government that works very well in practice, despite a mostly absent monarch.

The Governor General is a central constitutional actor in the framework of national government in Canada and largely fulfills the role of the monarch in the United Kingdom, where the monarch is a resident Sovereign. However, in constitutional terms, the Governor General is not a viceroy who fully occupies the role of the monarch in Canada. The Governor General remains an ordinary subject of the King or Queen like any other Canadian citizen and is not immune from the application of the law.

Over time there have been certain efforts, primarily by pockets of republicanism in the body politic of Canada, to grant the Governor General the dignity of recognition as the head of state of Canada. The difficulty faced by those who would wish to promote the Governor General from being the representative of a monarch who embodies the sovereignty of the country to be themselves the embodiment of Canadian sovereignty is that such a change would require a constitutional amendment consented to by each house of the Parliament and each provincial legislative assembly. Most astute observers feel that either the bar is too high for that to occur or the price to be paid to achieve it in terms of transferring the additional powers to the provinces sought by them as the political price for obtaining their necessary consent would be too high to contemplate. So the country remains, as it was at confederation in 1867, a constitutional monarchy with an overseas monarch as head of state.

That has not stopped republicans from trying to change the constitutional framework however, and around the turn of this century, a concerted effort was seen to have been made to supplant the monarch with the Governor General in the country's precedential order. Those efforts caused consternation in certain quarters of the country. The issue spanned the terms of office to two Governors General, Adrienne Clarkson, and Michaëlle Jean. Both women were appointed by a Liberal Ministry and both were what might be termed celebrity appointments, as both were well-known media personalities with extensive broadcasting careers at the Canadian Broadcasting Corporation, or Radio Canada, before their appointments.

Both Madame Clarkson and Madame Jean, as celebrity media personalities, knew how to claim the limelight and, as Governors General, both of them were widely acclaimed for injecting sparkle into what was otherwise considered to be a very drab public office. But their efforts to lay claim to head of state status caused uproar and seemed to reflect badly upon them and upon the officials who were assumed to be guiding their efforts.

The most serious incident revolved around the ceremonies marking the 60th anniversary of the Allied landings in Normandy during World War II. A large international commemoration was planned for this important historic event and Canada was expected to be a prominent part of the commemoration because Canadian troops took Juno Beach, one of the five landing beaches in Normandy on D-Day, June 6, 1944. Both Queen Elizabeth II and Governor General Clarkson were scheduled to attend this important ceremony but before Governor General Clarkson departed from Canada for France the staff at Rideau Hall, Canada's Government House, issued a press release stating that the Governor General would attend the ceremony in her capacity as Canada's head of state, which was wrong in the view of many constitutional experts. Furthermore, in the protocol for the ceremony at Juno Beach, the Queen was placed third in precedence behind both the Governor General and the Governor General's spouse, an act which insulted the Queen.[1] Afterward, under pressure, Rideau Hall clarified its statement that the Governor General was attending as head of state by withdrawing the suggestion and blaming a junior civil servant for the *faux pas*. However, there were no public amends for the displacement of the Sovereign in the order of precedence for the important international ceremony at Juno Beach in France.

Further, it appears from an interview that Clarkson gave after her term of office ended that she may have bought into a very

---

1. Historian J. L. Granatstein described the Royal Court as furious. See *Re: Adrienne Clarkson* - Alchetron, The Free Social Encyclopedia, https://alchetron.com/Adrienne-Clarkson. [accessed July 26, 2024]; *Canadian Confusion on Juno Beach*, https://web.archive.org/web/20131114134201/ http://www.monarchist.ca/sites/default/files/documents/2004/8/135.pdf

dubious constitutional theory popular in some Liberal party circles which held that the office of the Governor General had evolved sufficiently in the intervening years since confederation to enable the government to conclude that the Governor General now represented the "crown" directly, and was no longer the mere representative of the monarch.[2] The underlying conceptual theory seemed to be that the monarchy was external to the government of the state and served as a form of external or historical validation. Many, probably most, constitutional specialists considered such a theory to be unmeritorious, as it contradicted several explicit provisions of the *Constitution Acts 1867-1982.*

It is quite likely, however, that the Governor General was encouraged or guided in her views on the relative precedence of the monarch and the Governor General by civil servants on her staff at Rideau Hall. Of more concern is the support that may have been given to Rideau Hall by the Prime Minister's Office ("PMO"), which is the partisan nerve centre of government, and perhaps the Privy Council Office ("PCO"), the neutral civil service body that supports the policy work of the Prime Minister. While the role of the PMO is overtly partisan the role of the PCO is not. Constitutional law, tradition, and principle should always concern the staff at the PCO but we are left to wonder at the extent to which the PCO attempted to restrain proposals to elevate the status of the Governor General above the monarch. What is even more uncertain is the extent to which Rideau Hall's initiative received support from Cabinet Ministers. In her memoir, *Heart Matters*, Madame Clarkson stated accurately, albeit concerning another controversy during her tenure, that a Governor General takes no important action <u>except</u> on the advice and directions of the Ministry.[3]

However, the relative precedence of the Governor General and

2. *Re: Adrienne Clarkson*, Alchetron, The Free Social Encyclopedia
3. Adrienne Clarkson, *Heart Matters*, Penguin Canada, 2007, p. 192

the Queen was not only an issue during the tenure of Madame Clarkson at Rideau Hall. Her successor, Governor General Michaëlle Jean also found herself embroiled in this subject, following in the wake of Madame Clarkson. At a speech delivered in Paris, France, to the United Nations Educational, Scientific and Cultural Organization (UNESCO) Madame Jean twice referred to herself as the head of state of Canada, which, if true, would mean the displacement or subordination of the Sovereign in the order of precedence in Canada. Madame Jean's comments sparked a reaction from the then Prime Minister, Stephen Harper, who made it clear that Queen Elizabeth II was the head of state of Canada and that the Governor General was the representative of the Sovereign in Canada.[4]

Disputes over the role and relative precedence of the monarch and the Governors General have receded in recent years and it seems to be largely accepted now, even in Liberal Party circles, that the head of state of Canada is the Sovereign, currently King Charles III. For a time, however, these disputes generated considerable media ink and some public consternation. There has also been some practical fallout from these events. Probably at the behest of the Royal Court, there have been no further examples of an event on foreign soil attended by both the Sovereign of Canada and the Governor General of Canada. Now, only one or the other is commonly present at these events. Thus, at the 90th-anniversary rededication of the Vimy Memorial in France Queen Elizabeth II presided but at the 100th-anniversary commemoration, Governor General David Johnson presided, accompanied by Prince William, and Prince Harry, who represented the Royal Family. At the 80th anniversary commemoration of D-Day in Normandy in 2024, Governor General Mary Simon presided and Prince William attended the Canadian ceremonies as the representative of the Royal Family, even though

4. Sources: The Globe and Mail, *Just who does Governor-General Michaëlle Jean think she is? Canada's head of state? The Queen's representative? Or a bit of both?*, Toronto, October 10, 2009; The Toronto Star, *Head of state, c'est moi? Some are not amused*, Toronto, Oct. 10, 2009.

King Charles III was also in Normandy for the event.[5] However, in domestic appearances, the Sovereign of Canada continues to appear with the Governor General, and there, at least, it is clear that as a matter of constitutional principle, the Sovereign has absolute precedence in Canada.

The other area of dispute over precedence that emerged in the early part of the twenty-first century concerned the relative precedence of the Governor General and the Lieutenant Governors of the provinces. It will be recalled that in the late nineteenth century, the courts had ruled that the Crown in right of a province acting within the provincial sphere of jurisdiction was equal to the Crown in right of Canada acting within the federal sphere of jurisdiction. For the subject of precedence that meant that in a provincial ceremony, i.e., one organized by a province and concerning provincial jurisdiction, it was the provincial Lieutenant Governor that represented the Sovereign notwithstanding the presence of the Governor General of Canada. Provincial tables of precedence nevertheless make allowance for the application of the federal rules of precedence in certain circumstances to avoid disputes, particularly where international visitors are present. However, such accommodations were not intended to undermine the principle that a provincial Lieutenant Governor takes precedence at a formal

---

5. This approach appears to be a consistent policy of the royal court. The Liberal Ministry of Paul Martin also removed references to the Queen from the letters of credence and letters of recall of Canadian diplomats and advised foreign governments to address the letters of credence and recall in respect of their own diplomatic representatives in Canada to the Governor General instead of Queen Elizabeth II. (News Release, Prime Minister Paul Martin, *Canada updates diplomatic practice, Ottawa*, December 29, 2004; source: https://epe.lac-bac.gc.ca/100/205/301/pco-bcp/website/06-10-10/www.pco-bcp.gc.ca/printer.asp@printerfriendly=1&language=e&page=archivemartin&sub=news-communiques&doc=news_release_20041229_368_e.htm [accessed August 29, 2024] When the Ministry of Stephen Harper succeeded the Martin Ministry afterward Harper offered to restore the name of the monarch to the credentials of Canadian diplomats and on the letters submitted by foreign diplomats but the Royal Court declined the offer surely to avoid becoming a political issue between competing political parties in Canada.

ceremony within his or her province concerning a matter subject to provincial jurisdiction.

Unfortunately, as a result of attempts of the late 1990s and early twenty-first century to promote the concept of the Governor General as the evolved head of state, officials at Rideau Hall pursued the goal of the Governor General's domestic precedence very aggressively with the provincial Lieutenant Governors' staffs and that caused a great deal of backlash as a result. Provincial officials complained that they felt browbeaten by their counterparts at Rideau Hall into accepting superior precedence for the Governor General at provincial ceremonies and that ran counter to both constitutional law and tradition.[6] In her memoirs Madame Clarkson is silent about these precedence battles and it may be that those disputes were never elevated to her level, or the level of her provincial counterparts, although she does appear to make one oblique reference to the issue in *Heart Matters* where she expresses frustration over the fact that Canada seems to have two formal protocol systems, one external and one internal.[7]

Possible Reforms to Precedence in Canada

As we approach the end of the first quarter of the twenty-first century the precedence disputes of an earlier era have receded. Though the country has been administered by both Conservative and Liberal Ministries in recent years there have been no further efforts to promote the idea of the Governor General holding precedence over the monarch, nor any further suggestions that the Governor General is Canada's head of state. The current website of the Governor General of Canada explicitly states that "His Majesty King Charles III is King of Canada and head of state. The Governor General is the representative of the

---

6. *Adrienne Clarkson* - Alchetron, The Free Social Encyclopedia,
   https://alchetron.com/Adrienne-Clarkson. [accessed July 26, 2024]

7. *Heart Matters*, p. 239

King in Canada."[8] The consequence of that for state precedence now seems clear.

Nevertheless, there is scope for some reform to Canada's Table of Precedence to forestall precedence disputes from arising again in the future. The model for the contemporary Table of Precedence originated in the eighteenth and nineteenth centuries, as this work has shown. During those periods there were no examples of intermittent visits of a monarch to Canada. Therefore, the absence of the Sovereign from the Table of Precedence was not an oversight. Rather, a visit of the monarch to Canada was simply not envisaged during those early times. The vagaries and difficulties of transportation rendered it too risky for a monarch to embark on a major overseas trip. In modern times, however, Sovereigns of Canada have visited the country fairly frequently, as have other members of the Royal Family. Given that the monarchy does now have an occasional presence in the country It is surely time to update the national Table of Precedence to appropriately incorporate both the Sovereign and other members of the Royal Family into the Table of Precedence. The Tables of Precedence of two provinces, Newfoundland and Labrador, and Saskatchewan, now refer explicitly to the Sovereign in their respective tables. It would at least be very desirable for the federal Table of Precedence to place the Sovereign at the head of the federal Table of Precedence, consistent with the Sovereign's position as the head of state. In that way, any future issues over the relative precedence of the Sovereign and the Governor General, whether internationally or domestically, would be rendered moot.

Another change that is worth considering is to incorporate language into the federal table to provide flexibility where a particular ceremony is wholly or largely an issue of provincial

8. The Governor General of Canada, *Roles and Responsibilities*, https://www.gg.ca/en/governor-general [accessed August 9, 2024]

jurisdiction to allow a provincial table of precedence to apply to those particular circumstances. Some of the provincial tables of precedence make allowances for the possible application of the federal table in certain circumstances and a degree of reciprocity on the part of the federal government would serve to encourage collaboration between the respective federal and provincial government houses and serve as a symbol of cooperative federalism.

PART II.

_____

PART TWO - THE LAW OF
TITLES IN CANADA

_____

CHAPTER 10.

TITLES IN CANADA

The Sovereign is the fountain of honour and possesses the right to create all manner of dignities including titles, peerages, and knighthoods as part of the royal prerogative.

Post-Confederation Table of Titles

Shortly after confederation in 1867, and in conjunction with the approval of a Table of Precedence for Canada, a Table of Titles was also approved by Queen Victoria in July 1868. The first post-confederation Table of Titles set out certain official titles approved for use in Canada:

Table of Titles to be used in Canada, 1868[1]

• The Governor-General of Canada to be styled "His Excellency"

• The lieutenant governors of the provinces to be styled "his Honour"

• The privy councillors of Canada to be styled "Honourable," and for life[2]

• Senators of Canada, executive councillors of the provinces, the president of the Legislative Councils, and the Speakers of

1. Alpheus Todd, *Parliamentary Government in the British Colonies*, London, Longman, Green & Co., 1880, pp. 231-32.

2. Todd states that the exclusion of the Speaker of the House of Commons from also possessing this honourific was an oversight and that the Speaker retained the title of "Honourable" through usage, despite the exclusion.

the Houses of Assembly in the provinces, to be severally styled "Honourable," but only during office*

* Legislative councillors of the colonial provinces were permitted to retain the title "Honourable" for life but legislative councillors of the provinces who were appointed following Confederation were deprived of the future use of that title.

_____

The Modern Table of Titles

From time to time the Crown in right of Canada has reissued the Table of Titles to be used in Canada under the powers of the royal prerogative.[3] The Table of Titles for Canada that is in force at the time of this writing is as follows:

Table of Titles to be used in Canada[4]

1. The governor general of Canada to be styled "Right Honourable" for life and to be styled "His/Her Excellency" and their spouse "His/Her Excellency", as the cases may be, while in office.

2. The lieutenant governor of a province to be styled "Honourable" for life and to be styled "His/Her Honour" and their spouse "His/Her Honour", as the cases may be, while in office.

3. The Prime Minister of Canada to be styled "Right Honourable" for life.

4. The Chief Justice of Canada to be styled "Right Honourable" for life.

5. Privy councillors of Canada to be styled "Honourable" for life.

3. Lordon, *Crown Law*, p. 103

4. As revised June 18, 1993, and February 13, 2023; Source: https://www.canada.ca/en/canadian-heritage/services/protocol-guidelines-special-event/table-titles-canada.html [accessed August 15, 2024]

6. Senators of Canada to be styled "Honourable" for life.

7. The Speaker of the House of Commons to be styled "Honourable" while in office.

8. The Commissioner of a Territory to be styled "Honourable" while in office.

9. Puisne judges of the Supreme Court of Canada and judges of the Federal Court and of the Tax Court of Canada as well as the judges of the under-mentioned Courts in the Provinces and Territories to be styled "Honourable" while in office:
a. Ontario:
i. The Court of Appeal and the Ontario Court of Justice (General Division)
b. Quebec:
i. The Court of Appeal and the Superior Court of Quebec
c. Nova Scotia:
i. The Court of Appeal and the Supreme Court of Nova Scotia
d. New Brunswick:
i. The Court of Appeal and the Court of King's Bench of New Brunswick
e. Manitoba:
i. The Court of Appeal and the Court of King's Bench of Manitoba
f. British Columbia:
i. The Court of Appeal and the Supreme Court of British Columbia
g. Prince Edward Island:
i. The Supreme Court of Prince Edward Island
h. Saskatchewan:
i. The Court of Appeal and the Court of King's Bench of Saskatchewan
i. Alberta:
i. The Court of Appeal and the Court of King's Bench of Alberta
j. Newfoundland:
i. The Supreme Court of Newfoundland

k. Northwest Territories:

i. The Supreme Court of Northwest Territories

l. Yukon Territory:

i. The Supreme Court of Yukon

m. Nunavut Territory:

i. The Nunavut Court of Justice

10. Presidents and speakers of Legislative Assemblies of the Provinces and Territories to be styled "Honourable" while in office.

11. Members of the Executive Councils of the Provinces and Territories to be styled "Honourable" while in office.

12. Judges of Provincial and Territorial Courts (appointed by the Provincial and Territorial Governments) to be styled "Honourable" while in office

13. The following are eligible to be granted permission by the governor general, in the name of His Majesty The King, to retain the title of "Honourable" after they have ceased to hold office:

a. Speakers of the House of Commons

b. Commissioners of Territories

c. Judges designated in item 9

14. The title "Right Honourable" is granted for life to the following eminent Canadian:

a. The Right Honourable Donald F. Mazankowski[5]

The titles set out in the above table are the only titles that are officially recognized in Canada by the Crown

Obsolete Titles Part I – The Canadian Nobility

---

5. The Right Honourable Donald Mazankowski was deceased on October 27, 2020, and his continued appearance in the Table of Titles in 2024 probably reflects the infrequency in which the Crown updates the table!

Peerages are inheritable titles of nobility awarded by the Crown for special services to the Crown, to the country, or to society.[6] In Canada, the Crown in right of Canada (i.e. the Federal government) can exercise this prerogative power within the realm of Canada.[7]

Although some Canadians were awarded peerages during the late colonial period[8] when Canada continued to be subject to the suzerainty of Great Britain[9] a national policy was developed in Canada during the period following World War One to bar Canadians from being awarded or receiving peerages and knighthoods. The new policy likely reflected the distemper of the times, with its general revulsion against the policies of the Imperial statesmen that had led the empire, including the dominions, into the maelstrom of the Great War.

The catalysing event for the development of this policy was the grant of a barony to the proprietor of a Montreal newspaper, Hugh Graham, who thereby became Lord Atholstan, an

6. There are now two types of peerages in the United Kingdom, the traditional hereditary peerage that is inheritable, and a life peerage, which is not inheritable. However, as the latter was created by statute in the twentieth century it does not form part of the royal prerogative and therefore any peerage created by the Crown in right of Canada would have to be an inheritable peerage. Absent legislation, the Sovereign cannot create a life peerage; *Wensleydale Peerage Case* (1856), 5 H.L.C., 958 (England, H.L.); as the powers of the royal prerogative are limited by the common law; *Case of Proclamations* (1611), 12 Co. Rep., 74 (England, K.B.).

7. Lordon, *Crown Law*, pp. 102-03

8. In addition to the grant of British peerages, Queen Victoria also gave recognition to one title granted by King Louis XIV of France and Navarre before the conquest, the Baron de Longueüil, whose descendants now reside in Britain. (See Montague-Smith, *Debrett's Correct Form*, Debrett's Peerage Limited/Headline Book Publishing, London, 1992, p. 107)

9. A handful of these peerages (all of which were baronies) were made on the advice and at the request of the Canadian government and so they were considered to be Canadian peerages. The British government also granted some peerages to persons born in or ordinarily residing in Canada during this period but those peerages are regarded as British peerages, rather than Canadian peerages.

action taken by King George V on the advice of his British Ministers despite the contrary advice of Canadian Prime Minister, Sir Robert Borden. The reform of Canadian titles was spearheaded by a member of parliament, W. F. Nickle M.P., the Member of Parliament for Kingston who proposed a resolution requesting that the King cease to award hereditary titles to Canadians. That resolution was adopted by the House of Commons in 1918 and was designed to specifically target the granting of peerages. In April of the following year, Nickle introduced another resolution calling upon the King to cease granting any titular honours whatsoever to Canadians, including knighthoods. That proposal was referred to a Special Committee on Honours and Titles where W.F. Nickle continued to play a key role.[10] While the Special Committee was deliberating and reporting on this subject Prime Minister Borden was absent at the Paris Peace Conference. Otherwise, he might have moulded the report somewhat to lessen its impact.

In their report, the Special Committee called on King George V to "refrain hereafter from conferring any title of honour or titular distinction upon any of your subjects domiciled or ordinarily resident in Canada ..." and "... by legislation or otherwise to ensure the extinction of an hereditary title of honour or titular distinction, dignity or title as a peer of the realm on the death of a person domiciled or ordinarily resident in Canada at present in enjoyment of an hereditary title or honour or titular distinction, dignity or title as a peer of the realm ...". One can only imagine the reaction of the notoriously bad-tempered King to the suggestion that he should revoke peerages that he had previously granted!

10. The historian C. P. Stacey recounts Sir Robert Borden's opinion that Nickle was prompted to campaign against titles because his father-in-law, the Principal of Queen's University in Kingston was not given a knighthood although knighthoods were given to the Principal of McGill University and the President of the University of Toronto (see C.P. Stacey, *Historical Documents of Canada; Volume V, The Arts of War and Peace, 1914-1945*, Macmillan of Canada, Toronto, 1972, p, 196 fn.

In the result, however, the King made no further grants of peerage to Canadians and, except for a brief resurrection of knighthoods by Prime Minister Bennett in the mid-thirties, no Canadian government has requested and advised the Sovereign to grant a title or dignity to a Canadian. None of the titles previously granted by the Sovereign were revoked, however. Over time, the persons holding Canadian peerages found it more convenient to reside in Britain than in Canada and/or they died without descendants to inherit their titles. Thus, the few extant "Canadian" titles are now held by citizens of the United Kingdom and do not need to be further considered in this work.

The British Crown has continued to occasionally grant peerages and knighthoods to Canadians for services that they have rendered to Britain, generally where those Canadians so honoured hold dual Canadian-British citizenship. That, however, has not been without controversy.[11] Where Canadians have been granted peerages in the nobility of the United Kingdom for services that they rendered to the United Kingdom the practice, in conformity with the principles of the Nickle Resolutions, is that they do not use their British titles in Canada, thus reserving the use of their titles for those occasions when they sojourn in the United Kingdom.[12] As a result, those people are not normally addressed by their peerage titles in Canada.

When a person who holds a British peerage or baronetcy emigrates to Canada and becomes a Canadian citizen their British peerage or baronetcy will not be formally recognized in Canada, and Canadians don't have to refer to them with the style of title or manner of address that a British peer or baronet would be entitled to receive in the United Kingdom. As a matter of social convention, however, as opposed to a social requirement, Canadians may wish to address a British peer or baronet in Canada by their title for business, or social purposes.

11. *Black v Canada (Prime Minister)*, [2001] 54 OR (3d) 215 (Ont. C.A.)

12. For example, the newspaper proprietor Lord Thomson of Fleet.

There is, of course, no bar to Canadians doing so where they do so voluntarily, and in such cases, the British practice pertaining to forms of address for peers should be consulted.

Obsolete Titles Part II – The Gentry

The Gentry, as it was imported into Canada from Great Britain, included the classes of people that were capable of sustaining themselves from the rents that accrued from large landowning, persons who were members of certain elite professions, such as the judiciary, the legal professions, and the military, and persons honoured by the Crown. The ranks of the gentry in Canada, in descending order, were baronets, knights, seigneurs,[13] esquires, and gentleman (or gentlewoman). Beneath them were the yeoman, an intermediate class between the gentry and the labouring and husbandry classes. These distinctions have almost entirely disappeared from the modern egalitarian Canadian society, the seigneurs by legislation in the nineteenth century and the other classifications by desuetude although some usages still linger in certain very specific contexts.

Canadian Baronetcies

A baronetcy is a minor form of nobility ranked below peerages in the common law. It is, however, a hereditary honour and the holders of it are entitled to use the prefix "Sir" or "Dame" and the post-nominal letters Bt. or Bart. after the name of a man or Btss. after the name of a woman.

As with peerages, the Nickle Resolutions expressed a Canadian national policy that Canadians should not be awarded hereditary titles and although baronetcies were granted by the British Crown up to the late Imperial period, the practice ceased after the Nickle Resolutions were adopted by the Canadian House of Commons in 1919.[14]

13. This class was a holdover from the colonial structure of New France

14. Exceptionally, King George V awarded a baronetcy to a Canadian in 1921,

At the time of writing it appears that the former Canadian baronetcies have now become virtually extinct or, as with the Canadian peerages, have now become assimilated to the British nobility and little further consideration needs to be given to them. Where, however, a Canadian baronetcy is still extant, and is held by a Canadian citizen, they may be addressed in the manner described above in correspondence. Where the title is used the holder of the title would be addressed as Sir if a man or Dame if a woman.

In centuries past there was a class of baronets created by the Scottish Crown known as Baronets of Nova Scotia, which was intended to foster the settlement of the Province of Nova Scotia from the British Isles. However, none of the Baronets of Nova Scotia settled in the Province of Nova Scotia and today all such baronets created by the Crown are considered to be Scottish baronets, and are not recognized as Canadian baronets.

Canadian Knighthoods

A Knight is a dignity awarded by the Crown for services to the Crown, the country, or society, that warrants special recognition. It is not a hereditary honour, unlike an aristocratic title, and therefore it cannot be passed down to descendants. The Nickle Resolutions of 1918-19, in their final form, called for an end to the grant of knighthoods to Canadians by the Sovereign of the United Kingdom and subsequently the practice of granting knighthoods ceased in Canada during the late Imperial period, although King George V, as the Sovereign of Canada, did grant a handful of knighthoods to Canadians in the mid-1930's at the request of Prime Minister Richard Bennett. But after 1935, no other Canadian Ministry has recommended to the Sovereign that knighthoods be granted to Canadian citizens. Canadian knighthoods have now disappeared with the

which should perhaps be regarded as a transitional award during a period in which the national policy bar against titles being granted to Canadians was being implemented. No further baronetcies were subsequently conferred.

passage of time and therefore no special form of address for knights is required in Canada. Concerning British knights the British practice pertaining to forms of address for knights and Dames should be consulted should a Canadian wish to recognize the possession of a knighthood by a British citizen.

Seigneurs

The seigneurial system was established in New France to help populate the colony. Seigneurs held large estates which they divided and rented out to tenant farmers. The Seigneur was a prominent local citizen and from his tenants, called habitants, he could receive rents, compulsory labour, and levies on grain, woodcutting, hunting, and fishing.[15] This relationship between the seigneur, as 'lord of the manor', and his tenant farmers, in certain aspects, approximated a feudal relationship. The potential harms that characterize such relationships led to calls for the abolition of the seigneurial system, which ultimately occurred in 1854, long after the termination of French sovereignty in Canada.

Esquires

An Esquire is a gentry rank originating in the middle ages as the attendant of a knight but the rank came to be associated with the sons of peers, or the first son of a baronet or knight. Still later it became associated with certain elite professions that were closely associated with the Crown, or government. Those professions included the judiciary, the legal professions, and the officer ranks of the military. The status of an esquire was not exclusive, however, and certain other gentlemen might also be defined as an esquire in society. Historically, the rank was never applied to females and there was no equivalent rank for a female.

15. Source: https://www.thecanadianencyclopedia.ca/en/article/*seigneurial-system* [accessed August 15, 2024]

At present, the honourific of esquire is most commonly used within the legal professions and the judiciary although it has largely fallen out of favour in the more egalitarian society of modern times, particularly after the Law Society of Upper Canada, which is the largest organized provincial Bar in Canada, ceased to use this distinction in corresponding with its (male) members in 1990. The Law Society changed much of its nomenclature at that time to reflect the widespread influx of female lawyers into the profession by adopting gender-neutral language.[16] Nevertheless, the title is still used sometimes in correspondence between legal professionals, and it is also sometimes applied to certain minor judicial officers, such as a prothonotary.

Gentleman (or Gentlewoman)

The status of a gentleman (or gentlewoman) rested below the rank of esquire but the criteria for determining that status was even more unclear than the criteria for establishing who was entitled to be addressed as an esquire. Certain professions and academic appointments qualified a person as a gentleman or gentlewoman, as would the possession of a coat of arms granted or recognized by the Crown but this category of gentry was broader than that. In today's egalitarian society, however, everyone is presumptively a gentleman or gentlewoman unless their public conduct suggests otherwise.

Other Titles

Aboriginal Titles

Some aboriginal First Nations possess Hereditary Chiefs, particularly in the far western part of the country. The titles of Hereditary Chiefs are not officially recognized by the Federal

16. Curiously, in the United States, the title of esquire was retained within the legal profession and it is still often used by American attorneys, both male and female.

government, which recognizes only aboriginal Chiefs who have been elected to office. However, Hereditary Chiefs are at least officially acknowledged, as they often exert significant influence and even political power within particular First Nations. They are known collectively as Hereditary Chiefs in the English language although their particular title will always be derived from one of the aboriginal languages.[17]

Non-Titular Hereditary Dignities

Colonial Loyalist Honours

After the War of the American Revolution, many Americans who remained loyal to the Crown found it to be impossible to remain in the United States owing to the political conditions in the various states following the American success in the war and the establishment of independence. Therefore, many loyalist Americans fled to Canada as refugees where they were welcomed within the remaining boundaries of British North America. As a special recognition of their loyalty, the Crown, through Lord Dorchester, the Governor General of British North America, created a unique Canadian honour for the loyalists. Those persons who came to Canada as loyalists, together with their descendants were given the right to append the post-nominal letters of U.E., meaning "United Empire" after their names.[18] Although now infrequently used, the honour is still

17. For example, in the Huu-ay-aht First Nation of British Columbia the Hereditary Chief is known as the *ha'wiih*.

18. The definition of a loyalist according to the website of the United Empire Loyalist Association of Canada is a person "male or female, as of 19 April 1775, a resident of the American colonies, and joined the Royal Standard prior to the Treaty of Separation of 1783, or otherwise demonstrated loyalty to the Crown, and settled in territory remaining under the rule of the Crown; or a soldier who served in an American Loyalist Regiment and was disbanded in Canada; or a member of the Six Nations of either the Grand River or the Bay of Quinte Reserve who is descended from one whose migration was similar to that of other Loyalists."(see:https://uelac.ca/about/membership/ [accessed September 2, 2024)

customarily acknowledged where a descendant of a loyalist chooses to use the post-nominal letters. Note that the correct post-nominal letters granted to the descendants of loyalists are U.E. and not U.E.L. as it is sometimes rendered. The latter designation only applied to the original grantees.

Armigers

An armiger is a person who has received from the Crown certain heraldic emblems such as a coat of arms, or a flag, pennant, or badge, as a grant of honour in recognition of their contributions to the country.[19] A person who has received heraldic emblems from the Crown is entitled to display their arms publicly, or on letterhead, business cards, etc. However, the grant of arms to a person does not confer any titles or post-nominal letters. Heraldic emblems are considered to be a dignity granted by the Crown however, and they may also be a form of incorporeal heritable property. Persons who have received a grant of arms from the Crown may protect their arms by registering them and enforcing them under the provisions of the *Trademarks Act*.[20] Coats of Arms and other heraldic emblems are inheritable and pass by descent from the original grantee to their descendants.[21]

Possible Reform of the Table of Titles

Overall, Canadian titles have not proved to be controversial. However, it is curious in the twenty-first century that the Table of Titles, which is the formal expression of the honourifics applicable to the major offices of state in the country, does not contain any of the royal titles used by the Sovereign and the other members of the Royal Family. The absence of the royal titles from the official Table of Titles may suggest a view of the

19. Office of the Governor General of Canada, *The Canadian Heraldic Authority*, Rideau Hall, Ottawa, 1990, p. 15.

20. R.S.C., 1985, c. T-13, s.9 (1) (n.1)

21. Lordon, *Crown Law*, p. 100

monarchy as an externality, rather than as an integral aspect of the constitutional structure of the state. The Department of Canadian Heritage does provide guidance concerning the manner and form of address to use when Canadians interact with members of the Royal Family but it may be desirable, nevertheless, to include that guidance concerning the royal titles and forms of address along with the other high officials of the state within the Table of Titles to be used in Canada.

PART III.

_____

PART THREE - FORMS OF ADDRESS IN CANADA

_____

The forms of address contained in this part are largely a matter of custom, rather than law. I have been informed by the guidance offered by the many experts in this field and I have concurred with much of what I have discovered in their approaches. However, I have also made adjustments and changes where I have thought it to be fit and proper to do so.

Any obvious errors are, of course, entirely my own.

CHAPTER 11.

LIST OF DIGNITARIES IN PART THREE

THE ROYAL FAMILY

1. The Sovereign
2. The Consort of the Canadian Sovereign
3. The Heir Apparent to the Canadian Throne
4. Royal Dukes and Duchesses
5. Other Members of the Royal Family
6. The Private Secretary to the Sovereign
7. The Canadian Secretary to the Sovereign
8. The Governor General of Canada
9. The Governor General Designate of Canada
10. The Spouse of a Governor General of Canada
11. Former Governors General of Canada
12. The Spouse of a former Governor General of Canada
13. The Deputy of the Governor General of Canada
14. The Secretary to the Governor General of Canada
15. The Chief Herald of Canada
16. Other Household Officials
17. The Lieutenant Governor of a Province
18. The Lieutenant Governor Designate of a Province
19. The Spouse of a Lieutenant Governor of a Province
20. Former Lieutenant Governors of a Province
21. The Spouse of a former Lieutenant Governor of a Province
22. The Household Officials of the Lieutenant Governors
23. The Administrator of Canada
24. The Administrator of a Province

THE FEDERAL EXECUTIVE

25. Privy Councillors
26. The spouse of a Privy Councillor
27. The Prime Minister
28. The spouse of a Prime Minister
29. Former Prime Ministers
30. The spouse of a former Prime Minister
31. The President of the King's/Queen's Privy Council for Canada
32. Ministers Without Portfolio
33. Minister of a Department
34. Associate Ministers of a Department
35. Ministers of State
36. Territorial Commissioners
37. Deputy Commissioners
38. The Administrator of a Territory

THE PARLIAMENT OF CANADA

39. The Speaker of the Senate
40. The Speaker of the House of Commons
41. Senators
42. Parliamentary Secretaries
43. Members of Parliament
44. Clerk of the Senate and Clerk of the Parliaments
45. The Usher of the Black Rod
46. Law Clerk and Parliamentary Counsel
47. Clerk of the House of Commons
48. Dominion Offices

THE PROVINCIAL EXECUTIVES

49. Executive Councillors
50. The Premier
51. The Spouse of a Premier
52. Former Premiers
53. The Spouse of a Former Premier

54. Provincial Ministers
55. Former Provincial Ministers

THE PROVINCIAL LEGISLATURES

56. The Speaker of a Provincial Legislature
57. Members of a Provincial Legislature

THE TERRITORIAL EXECUTIVES

58. The Premier
59. The Spouse of a Premier of a Territory
60. Former Premiers
61. The Spouse of a Former Premier
62. Territorial Ministers

THE TERRITORIAL LEGISLATURES

63. The Speaker of a Territorial Legislature
64. Members of a Territorial Legislature

THE PUBLIC SERVICES

65. Public Servants

THE ARMED FORCES

66. Armed Forces Personnel

LOCAL GOVERNMENT AND ABORIGINAL FIRST NATIONS

67. Mayors
68. Wardens and Reeves
69. Members of Municipal Councils
70. First Nation Reserve Chiefs
71. Members of a First Nation Band Council

THE JUDICIARY AND THE LEGAL PROFESSION

72. The Chief Justice of Canada

73. Justices of the Supreme Court of Canada

74. The Registrar of the Supreme Court of Canada

75. Justices of a Provincial or Territorial Superior Court

76. Justices and Judges of the Federal Court, Federal Court of Appeal, Tax Court of Canada, or the Court Martial Appeal Court

Addressing Judicial Officers in Court

77. Addressing the Chief Justice of Canada in a Court Proceeding

78. Addressing a Justice of the Supreme Court of Canada in a Court Proceeding

79. Addressing the Registrar of the Supreme Court of Canada in a Court Proceeding

80. Addressing a Justice of one of the Federal Courts of Canada in a Court Proceeding

81. Newfoundland and Labrador Courts

82. Prince Edward Island Courts

83. Nova Scotia Courts

84. New Brunswick Courts

85. Quebec Courts

86. Ontario Courts

87. Manitoba Courts

88. Saskatchewan Courts

89. Alberta Courts

90. British Columbia Courts

91. Yukon Courts

92. Northwest Territories Courts

93. Nunavut Courts

94. Lawyers

THE DIPLOMATIC CORPS

95. Ambassadors, High Commissioners or Nuncios

CHAPTER 12.

FORMS AND STYLES OF ADDRESS IN CANADA

THE ROYAL FAMILY

1. The Sovereign

The Canadian Sovereign's Royal Style and Title[1]

The formal Canadian title of the Sovereign is established for each reign by a statute of the Canadian Parliament.[2] The Royal Style and Title is generally used only in the most formal legal documents, such as a Royal Proclamation. The current Canadian statute establishing the Canadian Sovereign's formal title is the *Royal Style and Titles Act, 2023.*[3] The formal title of the current Sovereign, King Charles III, is as follows:

Charles the Third, by the Grace of God King of Canada and His other Realms and Territories, Head of the Commonwealth.[4]

1. The formal royal style and title is generally used only in the most formal legal documents.

2. Certain conventions of the Commonwealth of Nations restrict the form of the title in each of the Commonwealth realms for which the British Monarch is the head of state to maintain a commonality in the title of the Sovereign across the Commonwealth. The three elements that must appear in the royal style and title according to the conventions of the Commonwealth of Nations are a reference to the monarch as Queen or King, a reference to the other realms of the monarch, and a reference to the position of the monarch as the Head of the Commonwealth. Otherwise, each of the Commonwealth realms may adapt a title for the Sovereign that is suitable for that country according to their own national needs.

3. S.C. 2023, c. 26, s. 510.

4. Before the independence of India, British monarchs from Queen Victoria to King George VI also held the higher title of Emperor (Empress, in the case of

Description of the Sovereign in Federal and Provincial Capacities.

In legal documents, a special formulation has been devised to differentiate the King acting in a federal capacity and the King acting in a provincial capacity. This subject is more fully elaborated in the appendices.[5]

Addressing the Sovereign in Person

When appearing before the Sovereign of Canada, Canadians should refer to the Sovereign firstly as *Your Majesty*, and thereafter as *Sir* if the Sovereign is a man or *Ma'am*, if the Sovereign is a woman.

Correspondence With the Sovereign

Correspondence with His Majesty the King should be addressed as follows:

> His Majesty The King [6][7]
> Buckingham Palace
> London SW1A 1AA
> United Kingdom
>
> The beginning salutation in a letter:
>
> *Your Majesty*
>
> The closing salutation in a letter:

Queen Victoria) of India. The title of Emperor of India, which was also used in the Royal Style and Title of the Sovereign in Canada, lapsed upon the independence of India and the cessation of the Indian Empire in 1947.

5. Infra, see Appendix B

6. Note: the name of the realm is not placed within the address. Therefore one does not address a letter to the King of Canada, or the King of the United Kingdom.

7. If a woman is the Sovereign substitute "Queen" for "King" in the address.

1) For Canadian subjects (citizens):

I remain Your Majesty's faithful and devoted servant,

2) Non-Canadians may close with either:

Respectfully,

or

Respectfully Yours,

2. The Consort of the Sovereign

Royal Style and Title

The Royal Style and Title of the consort of the Sovereign is established by the Sovereign exercising a royal prerogative power in accordance with the customs and practices of the Court of St. James's, which is the Royal Court of the United Kingdom.

Traditionally, a female consort will be given the title of Queen. There is no traditional title for a male consort and the practices of the Royal Court vary but recent practice has been to give a male consort the title of a Duke of the United Kingdom as a minimum and he may also be given the title of Prince.[8]

The Royal Style and Title of the current consort of the Sovereign is:

Her Majesty The Queen Consort

Addressing the Consort in Person

---

8. HRH Prince Philip was given the titles of Duke of Edinburgh, Earl of Merioneth and Baron Greenwich by HM King George VI shortly before his marriage to the then Princess Elizabeth. He was subsequently conferred with the title of Prince of the United Kingdom by HM Queen Elizabeth II.

When appearing before a female consort, Canadians should refer to her firstly as *Your Majesty* and thereafter as *Ma'am*.

When appearing before a male consort, Canadians should refer to him firstly as *Your Royal Highness* and thereafter as *Sir*.

In Correspondence

Correspondence with The Queen Consort should be addressed as follows:

> Her Majesty The Queen Consort
> Buckingham Palace
> London SW1A 1AA
> United Kingdom
>
> The beginning salutation in a letter to the Consort of a Canadian Sovereign:
>
> *Your Majesty* (if the consort is a female person possessing the title of Queen)
>
> *Your Royal Highness,* (if the consort is a male person)
>
> The closing salutation in a letter to the Consort of a Canadian Sovereign:
>
> *I remain Your Majesty's faithful and devoted servant,* (if the consort is a female person possessing the title of Queen)
>
> *Yours Very Truly,* (if the consort is a male person)

3. The Heir Apparent to the Canadian Throne

Royal Style and Title

The Royal Style and Title of the Heir Apparent or Heir Presumptive to the throne is established by the Sovereign exercising a royal prerogative power in accordance with the customs and practices of the Court of St. James's of the United Kingdom.

An Heir Apparent or Heiress Apparent (if female) is an heir to the throne whose position in the order of the succession cannot be displaced by the birth of a child to a reigning Sovereign. An Heir Presumptive, or Heiress Presumptive (if female) is an heir whose place in the order of succession can be displaced by the birth of a child to a reigning Sovereign. For example, the eldest niece or nephew of a reigning Sovereign can be an Heiress Presumptive or an Heir Presumptive, but they can be displaced if the Sovereign, or the spouse of the Sovereign, gives birth to a child.

Traditionally, a male heir apparent will receive the title of Prince of Wales when he has reached the age of majority. A female heiress apparent or heiress presumptive has not in the past been conferred with the title of Princess of Wales, which remains a title only conferred on the spouse of a Prince of Wales. However, the title of Princess Royal may be conferred upon a female Heiress Apparent, or Heiress Presumptive, according to the traditions of the royal court.

Addressing the Heir Apparent in Person:

When appearing before the heir apparent, or the heir presumptive to the throne, Canadians should refer to him or her firstly as *Your Royal Highness*, and thereafter as *Sir* (if a man) or *Ma'am* (if a woman).

In Correspondence:

> Correspondence with Prince William, The Prince of Wales should be addressed as follows:
>
> His Royal Highness The Prince of Wales
> Clarence House

London SW1A 1BA
United Kingdom

Correspondence with an Heir Apparent or Heir Presumptive who has not been conferred with the title of Prince of Wales should be addressed as follows:

His/Her Royal Highness, the Prince/Princess (insert name)

Correspondence with a female Heir Apparent or Heir Presumptive who has been conferred with the title of Princess Royal, or any member of the Royal Family upon whom the Sovereign has conferred the title of Princess Royal should be addressed as follows:

Her Royal Highness, the Princess Royal

For all persons who hold the status of Heir Apparent or Heir Presumptive to the Throne the opening and closing salutations of a letter should be as follows:

The beginning salutation in a letter:

Your Royal Highness,

The closing salutation in a letter:

Yours Very Truly,

4. Royal Dukes and Duchesses

A male member of the royal family may be conferred with the title of a Duke and thus become a Royal Duke. His wife thereby becomes a Royal Duchess.

Addressing a Royal Duke or a Royal Duchess in Person:[9]

When appearing before a Royal Duke Canadians should refer to him firstly as *Your Royal Highness* and thereafter as *Sir*.

When appearing before a Royal Duchess Canadians should refer to her firstly as *Your Royal Highness,* and thereafter as *Ma'am*.

In Correspondence:

Correspondence with a Royal Duke or Duchess should be addressed to their official residence in the United Kingdom but where they do not maintain an official residence in the United Kingdom or if it is unknown the correspondence should be addressed to Buckingham Palace as follows:

His/Her Royal Highness The Duke/Duchess of

————————————
Buckingham Palace
London SW1A 1AA
United Kingdom

The beginning salutation in a letter:

Your Royal Highness,[10]

The closing salutation in a letter:

Yours Very Truly,

5. Other Members of the Royal Family

9. At the present time some Royal Dukes and Duchesses have ceased to perform official duties and in such cases (e.g. the Duke and Duchess of Sussex, the Duke of York) this formal salutation should be omitted in favour of using the salutations of "Sir" or "Ma'am".

10. At present, some Royal Dukes and Duchesses have ceased to perform official duties and in such cases (e.g. the Duke and Duchess of Sussex, the Duke of York) this formal salutation should be omitted in favour of using the salutations of *Dear Sir* or *Dear Madam*.

Addressing Members of the Royal Family in Person Who Bear the Style His or Her Royal Highness:[11]

When appearing before a member of the Royal Family who is entitled to be addressed as His or Her Royal Highness Canadians should refer to them firstly as *Your Royal Highness*, and thereafter as *Sir* or *Ma'am*, as the occasion requires.

In Correspondence:

> His Royal Highness, The (Prince . . . or The Duke of . . .)
>
> > or
>
> Her Royal Highness, The (Princess . . . or The Duchess of . . .)
>
> The beginning salutation in a letter:
>
> *Your Royal Highness,*
>
> The closing salutation:
>
> *Yours Very Truly,*

Addressing Spouses of Members of the Royal Family who are entitled to the rank of His or Her Royal Highness

Where a person is the spouse of a member of the Royal Family

---

11. By letters patent issued in 1917, King George V commanded that henceforth the sons and daughters of the Sovereign would carry the His/Her Royal Highness style, as would the grandchildren in the male line of the Sovereigns. Beyond the grandchildren, only the eldest son of the eldest living son of the Prince of Wales would be entitled to the His Royal Highness style. As of 2012, this was changed so that all of the children of the eldest son of the Prince of Wales receive the His/Her Royal Highness designation. Those who are entitled to pass the His/Her Royal Highness designation to their children can request that it not be done. Those who are entitled to the His/Her Royal Highness title may voluntarily cease to use it if, for example, they withdraw from their official duties in connection with the Royal Family.

who is entitled to the rank of His or Her Royal Highness, that person may also be granted to right to be addressed as His or Her Royal Highness by the Sovereign. Where spouses of a member of the Royal Family who have been granted the rank of HRH subsequently become divorced, they will cease to possess the title of His or Her Royal Highness but are still referred to by the peerage title of nobility held by their former spouse.

Members of the Royal Family Who are Not Styled His or Her Royal Highness

The members of the Royal Family who are not entitled to the use of the honourific His or Her Royal Highness are to be addressed according to the formal title, if any, that they hold, or the courtesy title that they may use by custom, without the prefixes of "His Royal Highness" or "Her Royal Highness". For example:[12]

Correspondence With Members of the Royal Family Who Possess a Courtesy Title

"Lady Jane Windsor,"

or

"Viscount Shropshire,"

Correspondence With Members of the Royal Family Who Do Not Possess a Courtesy Title

"Ms. Samantha Mountbatten-Windsor,"

or

"Stephen Mountbatten-Windsor, Esq.,"

or

12. These are fictitious examples.

"Mr. Arthur Mountbatten-Windsor,"

The beginning salutation in a letter:

Dear Lady Jane Windsor,

or

Dear Viscount Shropshire

or

Dear Ms. Samantha Mountbatten-Windsor

or

Dear Stephen Mountbatten-Windsor,

The closing salutation in a letter:

Yours Very Truly,

6. The Private Secretary to the Sovereign

The Sovereign's Private Secretary holds the most senior operational position within the Royal Household and is the principal advisor to the Sovereign on matters of constitutional law, political questions, and matters of government practice in the United Kingdom and in the Commonwealth realms for which the Sovereign acts as the head of state. The Private Secretary is responsible for the Sovereign's correspondence and papers and coordinates the Sovereign's official program.

For those Canadians who wish to forward some intelligence to the Sovereign, or who prefer to correspond with the monarch in the most formal manner, it is suggested that they may wish to communicate through the Private Secretary.

Formal Title

The Private Secretary to the King (or Queen, if a female person ascends the throne)

In Correspondence

> The Private Secretary to the King/Queen
> Buckingham Palace
> London SW1A 1AA
> United Kingdom

The beginning salutation in a letter:

Dear Sir (or Dear Madam, is the post is held by a woman)

The closing salutation in a letter:

Yours Truly,

7. The Canadian Secretary to the Sovereign

The office of the Canadian Secretary to the King (or Queen, if a female person ascends the Throne) is not the Canadian counterpart to the Private Secretary to the King at Buckingham Palace. Rather, the Canadian office, first established in 1959, is primarily an office which acts as an interlocutor between the Canadian Government and the Royal Household.[13] As such, its services are primarily internal within the Government of Canada. The Canadian Secretary to the King does not manage correspondence addressed to the King of Canada. Therefore, formal correspondence from Canadians to His Majesty the King (where the correspondent chooses not to address their letter directly to the Sovereign) should be addressed to the Private Secretary to the King at Buckingham Palace in the United Kingdom. Where it is necessary to correspond with the Cana-

---

13. *After years of mixed messages, Trudeau signals he's treating the Crown more seriously,* National Post, December 9, 2019

dian Secretary to the King the form suggested below for Public Servants should be consulted.

THE VICE REGAL ESTABLISHMENTS

Canada is a constitutional monarchy without a resident monarch. Like fourteen other former British colonies, Canada has retained the Sovereign of the United Kingdom of Great Britain and Northern Ireland as its own constitutional monarch. While the King or Queen is resident in the United Kingdom the work of government in Canada, and in its provinces, requires that a representative of the Sovereign be present in Canada to carry out the functions of the monarch, according to constitutional principles. Early in the colonial period, this representative function was fulfilled by a person appointed by the monarch as their representative, commonly, though not always formally described, as the Governor General of Canada. Samuel de Champlain is considered to have been the first Governor General and the office was held by French-born nobility until the appointment in 1755 of Pierre de Rigaud, Marquis de Vaudreuil, the last Governor General under the Kings of France. The Marquis de Vaudreuil was Canadian-born, (as well as the son of a previous Governor General). Subsequently, the office of Governor General was held by British nobility until the appointment of Vincent Massey, a Canadian citizen, in 1952. Since 1952 all appointments to the office have been held by Canadian citizens.

In addition to the appointment of a Governor General to represent the Sovereign in Canada, the confederation of the Canadian provinces in 1867 led to a requirement for separate representatives of the Sovereign to be appointed to discharge the functions of the constitutional monarch within the provinces, under the title and style of the Lieutenant Governor (pronounced "Leftenant Governor" in Canada).

Although the Governor General and the Lieutenant Governors

are described as vice-regal appointees they are not Viceroys in the full legal sense of that word, and as citizens, they remain ordinary subjects of the King of Canada and are subject to all of the public and civil laws of Canada in the discharge of their offices, or the conduct of their personal lives.

8. The Governor General of Canada

The Governor General of Canada is the representative of the Sovereign of Canada within the country and holds the second-highest office in the structure of the Canadian government. The Governor General's main function is to ensure that a constitutional government is always in place and is capable of carrying out the functions of governance in Canada at all times. The Governor General will also open, prorogue, and dissolve Parliament and will exercise the royal power to grant Royal Assent to legislation passed by the Parliament of Canada, a necessary step for a law to take effect. The Governor General also exercises the Sovereign's royal prerogative powers in Canada, where such powers fall within federal jurisdiction, including the prerogative powers of appointment, and the grant of precedence, dignities and honours to Canadians. Additionally, the Governor General carries out many symbolic functions that contribute to recognition and national unity, and may represent Canada abroad during state visits to other countries.

The Canadian Governor General's Vice-Regal Style and Title

Governor General and Commander-in-Chief in and over Canada

For descriptive purposes, the formal Vice-Regal Style and Title is rendered less cumbersomely by the Government of Canada as:

Governor General and Commander-in-Chief of Canada

As in the case of the Sovereign, the use of the formal Vice-Regal Style and Title is generally restricted to formal legal documents, for example, proclamations and commissions or the like.

The Governor General's Honourific Titles

A Governor General of Canada is entitled to the prefix title of *Your Excellency* and honourific title of *The Right Honourable* before their name in correspondence. The Governor General retains the prefix title only during their term of office but the honourific title of *The Right Honourable* is kept by them for life.

Addressing the Governor General in Person

When appearing before the Governor General of Canada, Canadians should refer to the Governor General firstly as *Your Excellency*, or *Excellency*, and thereafter as *Ma'am*, if the Governor General is a woman, or *Sir* if the Governor General is a man. The Governor General is not referred to in conversation by their title of office (i.e., they are not called Governor or Governor General in conversation)

Correspondence With the Governor General of Canada

Correspondence with the Governor General should be addressed as follows:

(Female Governor General)

Her Excellency the Right Honourable . . . C.C., C.M.M., C.O.M, C.D.[14]
Governor General of Canada
Rideau Hall
1 Sussex Drive Ottawa, Ontario
K1A 0A1

or

14. All Governors General of Canada receive these post-nominal letters which represent Orders of State or decorations of honour

(Male Governor General)

His Excellency the Right Honourable . . . C.C., C.M.M., C.O.M, C.D.
Governor General of Canada
Rideau Hall
1 Sussex Drive Ottawa, Ontario
K1A 0A1

The beginning salutation in a letter:

Excellency:

The closing salutation in a letter:

Yours Truly,

9. The Governor General Designate of Canada

A person whose appointment as Governor General of Canada has been approved of by the King (or Queen) of Canada, and whose appointment has been publicly announced, should be referred to as the Governor General Designate of Canada. However, such persons are not entitled to use any prefix honourific (such as Your Excellency or The Right Honourable), that is associated with the office of the Governor General until they take the required oaths and formally assume that office. In the interim period, it is suggested that correspondence addressed to a Governor General Designate be sent to Rideau Hall, where the staff of the Office of the Governor General can hold or forward the correspondence to the incoming Governor General, as appropriate.

Correspondence with the Governor General Designate of Canada

Mr./M. . . .
Governor General Designate of Canada
Rideau Hall

1 Sussex Drive Ottawa, Ontario
K1A 0A1

or

Ms./Mrs./Mme. ....
Governor General Designate of Canada
Rideau Hall
1 Sussex Drive Ottawa, Ontario
K1A 0A1

The beginning salutation in a letter:

Dear Sir:

or

Dear Madam:

The closing salutation in a letter:

Yours Truly,

10. The Spouse of a Governor General of Canada

The spouse of a Governor General who is otherwise not titled has been granted the privilege of using the prefix title of *Your Excellency* as an honourific since 1924.

Addressing the Spouse of a Governor General in Person

When appearing before the spouse of a Governor General of Canada, Canadians should refer to the Governor General's spouse firstly as *Your Excellency*, or *Excellency*, and thereafter as *Ma'am*, if the Governor General's spouse is a woman, or *Sir*, if the Governor General's spouse is a man.

Correspondence With the Spouse of a Governor General of Canada

Correspondence with the spouse of a Governor General should be addressed as follows:

(Female spouse of a Governor General)

Her Excellency (Ms./ Mrs./Mme.) . . . C.C.[15]
Rideau Hall
1 Sussex Drive Ottawa, Ontario
K1A 0A1

or

(Male spouse of a Governor General)

His Excellency (Mr./M.) . . . C.C.
Rideau Hall
1 Sussex Drive Ottawa, Ontario
K1A 0A1

The beginning salutation in a letter:

Excellency:

The closing salutation in a letter:

Yours Truly,

11. Former Governors General of Canada

A former Governor General of Canada is entitled to retain the honourific title of *The Right Honourable* for life and should be addressed as such in correspondence. However, once they cease to hold the office of Governor General, they are no longer addressed as Your Excellency or Excellency.

Addressing a former Governor General in Person

A former Governor General of Canada remains an ordinary

---

15. All spouses of Governors General of Canada receive these post-nominal letters which represent the Order of Canada.

citizen and subject of the Sovereign and should be addressed in the same manner as any other Canadian should be addressed in appropriate social contexts. Depending on the circumstances, and the relationship between the speakers, a former Governor General of Canada should be addressed as, for example, *Mr.* Smith or *Ms.* Smith. Where the circumstances are very formal, or there is a great age disparity between the speakers the former Governor General may be addressed as *Sir* or *Ma'am*.

Correspondence With a Former Governor General of Canada

> The Right Honourable . . . C.C., C.M.M., C.O.M, C.D.[16]
> (Insert mailing address),
>
> The beginning salutation in a letter:
>
> *Dear Sir*:
>
> or
>
> *Dear Madam:*
>
> The closing salutation in a letter:
>
> *Yours Truly,*

12. The Spouse of a Former Governor General of Canada

The spouse of a former Governor General of Canada remains an ordinary citizen and subject of the Sovereign of Canada and, is treated in the same manner as any other citizen in Canada.

Addressing the Spouse of a Former Governor General in Person

---

16. Former Governors General retain these post-nominal letters after they cease to hold office.

The spouse of a former Governor General of Canada is no longer addressed as Your Excellency, or Excellency, once their spouse ceases to hold the office of Governor General. They are addressed in the same manner as others, for example, *Mr. Smith* or *Ms. Smith*. Where the circumstances are very formal, or there is a great age disparity between the speakers, the former Governor General may be addressed as *Sir* or *Ma'am*.

Correspondence With the Spouse of a Former Governor General of Canada

> Ms./Mrs./Mr. . . . C.C.,[17]
> (Insert mailing address)
>
> The beginning salutation in a letter:
>
> *Dear Sir*:
>
> or
>
> *Dear Madam:*
>
> The closing salutation in a letter:
>
> *Yours Truly,*

The Governor General's Household Officials

The Office of the Governor General of Canada is assisted or served by a number of senior officials in addition to the staff who serve the Governor General at the two official residences of the Governor General, Rideau Hall in Ottawa, and La Citadelle in Quebec City.

13. The Deputy of the Governor General of Canada

The Canadian Constitution provides that a Governor General

---

17. The spouses of former Governors General of Canada retain these post-nominal letters after their spouse ceases to hold office.

may appoint one or more persons to act as the Deputy of the Governor General and it has been the practice of Governors General to appoint deputies to assist them in the discharge of their office. Two types of deputies have been appointed. In the first category are the Chief Justice of Canada and the puisne Justices of the Supreme Court of Canada who are deputized to act when the Governor General is unavailable for some reason. The appointment of a deputy, or the exercise of the royal prerogative powers by a deputy, does not affect in any manner the exercise of those same powers by the Governor General.

Formerly, Supreme Court Justices acting as the Deputy of the Governor General frequently appeared in Parliament to grant Royal Assent to legislation but this practice has become rare because the Governor General now normally grants Royal Assent privately, without an appearance in Parliament. When the Chief Justice or a Justice of the Supreme Court acts as a Deputy of the Governor General it is normally an ephemeral duty that is limited in time and to a particular function. As such, the judicial officials are not acting as a full representative of the Sovereign but merely as a delegate of the Governor General. Under such circumstances the honourifics associated with the position of Governor General would not apply, and Canadians who are required to address a Chief Justice or Justice acting as the Deputy of the Governor General should address them with the titles and honours associated with their judicial office.

A second type of Deputy of the Governor General that is commonly appointed consists of officials employed in the Office of the Governor General of Canada to execute Crown legal instruments. The Secretary to the Governor General and other officials may be appointed as a Deputy of the Governor General for these limited purposes. This type of deputation is limited in scope and is a mere adjunct to their employment responsibilities. No special form of address should be used in connection with such officials and they should be addressed in the same manner as other public servants (see below *infra*).

Addressing the Chief Justice of Canada or a Justice of the Supreme Court of Canada acting as the Deputy of the Governor General of Canada

The Deputy should be addressed as *Chief Justice* if they hold that office, or as *Justice* if they are a puisne justice of the Supreme Court.

Correspondence with the Chief Justice of Canada or a Justice of the Supreme Court of Canada acting as the Deputy of the Governor General of Canada

Correspondence with a judicial Deputy of the Governor General of Canada should follow the forms suggested later in this text for the Chief Justice and Puisne Justices of the Supreme Court of Canada.

14. The Secretary to the Governor General of Canada

The Secretary to the Governor General holds the most senior operational position within Rideau Hall (Government House) and is the principal advisor to the Governor General on all matters of governance within the Canadian realm. All other officials in the Government House normally report to the Governor General through the Secretary and thus the Secretary has overall charge of the administration of the Governor General's Office. As such, the Secretary is responsible for the Governor General's correspondence and papers and coordinates the Governor General's official program. Where necessary, official communications between the Governor General and the Sovereign, or the Prime Minister, will be passed through the office of the Secretary to the Governor General.

Formal Title

The Secretary to the Governor General of Canada

Addressing the Secretary of the Governor General of Canada

The Secretary is addressed in person as *Sir* or *Ma'am*.

In Correspondence

> The Secretary to the Governor General of Canada
> Rideau Hall
> 1 Sussex Drive Ottawa, Ontario
> K1A 0A1

> The beginning salutation in a letter:

> *Dear Sir (or Dear Madam, is the post is held by a woman)*

> The closing salutation in a letter:

> *Yours Truly,*

15. The Chief Herald of Canada

The Chief Herald of Canada has the control and direction of the Canadian Heraldic Authority, the body that is responsible for exercising the Sovereign's royal prerogative to grant a coat of arms and other heraldic honours to Canadians.

Formal Title

Director, Canadian Heraldic Authority and Chief Herald of Canada;

Addressing the Chief Herald of Canada

There are no prefix titles or honourific associated with the position but in a formal setting, such as a Proclamation of Arms ceremony, the incumbent may be addressed by their title of office (i.e., they may be addressed, or referred to, as *Chief Herald*).

In Correspondence

> The Chief Herald of Canada
> Rideau Hall
> 1 Sussex Drive Ottawa, Ontario
> K1A 0A1
>
> The beginning salutation in a letter:
>
> *Dear Sir (or Dear Madam, is the post is held by a woman)*
>
> The closing salutation in a letter:
>
> *Yours Truly,*

16. Other Household Officials

There are no special rules respecting the form of address or style of title for other vice-regal household officials and they should be addressed, or corresponded with, in the same manner as one would address, or correspond, with any other public servant (see below, *infra*).

17. The Lieutenant Governor of a Province

The Lieutenant Governor of a Canadian province is a high vice-regal official serving in a capacity as the provincial head of state within the Canadian Confederation. Each province has a Lieutenant Governor at its head.

Primarily, the Lieutenant Governor serves as the representative of the Sovereign of Canada within a province and the duties of the Lieutenant Governor in that capacity mirror the responsibilities of the Governor General of Canada in respect to the country as a whole. Thus, as the Sovereign's representative within a province, each Lieutenant Governor will ensure that at all times a functioning government is in place within the province, he or she will open, prorogue, and dissolve the provincial legislature, and will exercise both the power to grant Royal Assent to legislation enacted by the legislative body within the province, and the royal prerogatives of the Sovereign that fall within provincial jurisdiction. The Lieutenant Governor will also attend public functions, make provincial awards, and generally carry out all of the ceremonial functions of the monarchy within their province.

The Lieutenant Governor's Vice-Regal Style and Title

Lieutenant Governor of the Province of. . . (e.g. Ontario, Quebec, New Brunswick, Nova Scotia, Manitoba, British Columbia, Prince Edward Island, Saskatchewan, Alberta, Newfoundland and Labrador)

The Lieutenant Governor's Honourific Titles

A Lieutenant Governor of a Canadian province is entitled to the prefix title of *Your Honour* and the honourific title of *The Honourable* before their name in correspondence. A Lieutenant Governor retains the prefix title *The Honourable* for life but they are only referred to as *Your Honour* during their term of office.

Addressing the Lieutenant Governor of a Province in Person

When appearing before a Lieutenant Governor of a Province of Canada, Canadians should refer to the Lieutenant Governor firstly as *Your Honour*, and thereafter as *Ma'am*, if the Lieutenant Governor is a woman, or *Sir* if the Lieutenant Governor is a man. The Lieutenant Governor is not referred to in conversation by their title of office (i.e., they should not be called Lieutenant Governor, or Governor, in conversation)

Correspondence with a Lieutenant Governor of a Province

Correspondence with a Lieutenant Governor should be addressed as follows:

(Female Lieutenant Governor)

Her Honour The Honourable (Insert the name and any post-nominal letters, if known)
Lieutenant Governor of (Insert the name of the Province)
mailing address (Insert the mailing address from the list in the appendix[18])

or

(Male Lieutenant Governor)

His Honour The Honourable (Insert the name and any post-nominal letters, if known)
Lieutenant Governor of (Insert the name of the Province)
mailing address (Insert the mailing address from the list in the appendix)

The beginning salutation in a letter:

Your Honour:

or

My dear Lieutenant Governor:

The closing salutation in a letter:

Yours Truly,

18. The Lieutenant Governor Designate of a Province

A person whose appointment as Lieutenant Governor of a Province has been approved by the Governor General of Canada, and whose appointment has been publicly announced, should be referred to as the Lieutenant Governor Designate of the Province to which he or she is appointed.

18. Refer to Appendix C

However, as with a Governor General Designate, a Lieutenant Governor Designate is not entitled to use any prefix honourific (such as Your Honour, or The Honourable, that is associated with the office of the Lieutenant Governor until they take the required oaths and formally assume their office. In the interim period, it is suggested that correspondence addressed to a Lieutenant Governor Designate be sent to the Office of the Lieutenant Governor for the Province in which they have been appointed, where the staff of the Office of the Lieutenant Governor can hold or forward the correspondence to the Lieutenant Governor Designate, as appropriate.

Correspondence with a Lieutenant Governor Designate of a Province

Mr. . . . (Insert the name and any post-nominal letters, if known)
Lieutenant Governor Designate of (Insert the name of the Province)
mailing address (Insert the mailing address from the list in the appendix)

or

Ms. . . . (Insert the name and any post-nominal letters, if known)
Lieutenant Governor Designate of (Insert the name of the Province)
mailing address (Insert the mailing address from the list in the appendix)

The beginning salutation in a letter:

Dear Sir:

or

Dear Madam:

The closing salutation in a letter:

Yours Truly,

19. The Spouse of a Lieutenant Governor of a Province

The spouse of a Lieutenant Governor who is otherwise not titled has the privilege of using the prefix title of *Your Honour* as an honourific during the term of office of their spouse.

Addressing the Spouse of a Lieutenant Governor in Person

When appearing before the spouse of a Lieutenant Governor of a Province, Canadians should refer to the Lieutenant Governor's spouse firstly as *Your Honour* and thereafter as *Ma'am*, if the Lieutenant Governor's spouse is a woman, or *Sir*, if the Lieutenant Governor's spouse is a man.

Correspondence With the Spouse of a Lieutenant Governor of a Province

Correspondence with the spouse of a Lieutenant Governor should be addressed as follows:

(Female spouse of a Lieutenant Governor)

Her Honour (Ms./Mrs./Mme.) . . . (Insert the name and any post-nominal letters, if known)
(Insert the mailing address from the list of Lieutenant Governor's offices in the appendix)

or

(Male spouse of a Lieutenant Governor)

His Honour (Mr./M.) . . . (Insert the name and any post-nominal letters, if known)
(Insert the mailing address from the list of Lieutenant Governor's offices above)

The beginning salutation in a letter:

Dear (Sir or Madam)

The closing salutation in a letter:

Yours Truly,

20. Former Lieutenant Governors of a Province

A former Lieutenant Governor of a Province is entitled to retain the honourific title of *The Honourable* for life and should be addressed as such in correspondence. However, once they cease to hold the office of a Lieutenant Governor, they are no longer addressed as Your Honour.

Addressing a former Lieutenant Governor in Person

A former Lieutenant Governor General of a Province remains an ordinary citizen and subject of the Canadian Sovereign and should be addressed in the same manner as any other Canadian would be addressed in appropriate social contexts. Depending on the circumstances, and the relationship between the speakers, a former Lieutenant Governor should be addressed as, for example, *Mr.* Smith or *Ms.* Smith. Where the circumstances are very formal, or there is a great age disparity between the speakers, the former Lieutenant Governor may be addressed as Sir or *Ma'am.*

Correspondence With a Former Lieutenant Governor General of a Province

> The Honourable . . . (Insert the name and any post-nominal letters, if known)
> (Insert personal address of the recipient)
>
> The beginning salutation in a letter:
>
> *Dear Sir:*

or

Dear Madam:

<u>The closing salutation in a letter:</u>

Yours Truly,

21. The Spouse of a Former Lieutenant Governor of a Canadian Province

The spouse of a former Lieutenant Governor of a Canadian province does not retain the right to use any honourific after their spouse ceases to hold the office of Lieutenant Governor and is addressed in the same manner as other citizens of Canada.

Addressing the Spouse of a Former Lieutenant Governor in Person

The spouse of a former Lieutenant Governor of a Canadian province is no longer addressed as Your Honour, once their spouse ceases to hold the office of Lieutenant Governor. They are addressed in the same manner as other citizens should be addressed, for example, as *Mr.* Smith or *Ms.* Smith. Where the circumstances are very formal, or there is a great age disparity between the speakers, the spouse of the former Lieutenant Governor may be addressed as *Sir* or *Ma'am*.

Correspondence With the Spouse of a Former Lieutenant Governor of a Canadian Province

Ms./Mrs./Mme./Mr./M./ . . . (Insert the name and any post-nominal letters, if known)
(Insert the personal address of the recipient)

<u>The beginning salutation in a letter:</u>

Dear Sir:

or

Dear Madam:

The closing salutation in a letter:

Yours Truly,

22. The Household Officials of the Lieutenant Governors

The Lieutenant Governors of all the Canadian Provinces are assisted by staff who address the requirements of their official programs and act as their chief advisors. In addition, some of the provinces maintain official residences for the Lieutenant Governor of the Province and in those cases, there will also be staff to maintain the physical household of the Lieutenant Governor.

The title and specific duties of the advisors to the Lieutenant Governors will vary by province and therefore inquiries may be made to ascertain the correct names and employment titles of the household official of a Lieutenant Governor that you wish to contact. Generally, there will be one senior official titled Secretary, or Chief of Staff, who is responsible for the business of the Lieutenant Governors Office, and there should also be a person who is the Honourary Aide-de-Camp to the Lieutenant Governor.

There are no special rules respecting the form of address or style of title for household officials and they should be addressed or corresponded with in the same manner as one would address or correspond with any other public servant except that an Honourary Aide-de-Camp is entitled to use the post-nominal letters A. de C., and those post-nominal letters should be appended to the name of the Aide-de-Camp in any correspondence.

The Office of the Administrator

In situations where a representative of the Sovereign of Canada is away from their jurisdiction, is incapacitated, or has died in office, the constitutional law and practice of Canada provides for an official to substitute for the absent, incapacitated, or deceased representative of the Crown. The class of officials who have been designated to perform this function are the members of the senior judiciary in Canada. At least formally, in Canada, the Sovereign is the head of the executive government, the head of the judiciary, as well as the highest branch of the Parliament and the Legislatures, so there is no formal breach of constitutional principles respecting the separation of powers by the appointment of judicial officers to act in the capacity of an Administrator. Such appointments, except in the case of incapacity, are normally of very brief duration and serve to ensure that the functions of government continue during the temporary unavailability of the representative of the Sovereign.

23. The Administrator of Canada

The office of the Administrator of Canada was created by section 10 of the *British North America Act* (now the *Constitution Act, 1867*[19]) and the office was vested in the Chief Justice, or puisne justices, of the Supreme Court of Canada by the *Letters Patent Constituting the Office of Governor General and Commander-in-Chief of Canada*, issued by King George VI on September 8, 1947[20]. In the case of the absence, incapacity or death of the Governor General of Canada the Chief Justice of Canada is designated to act in the place of the Governor General. If the Chief Justice is unavailable, or the office of Chief Justice is vacant, the puisne justices of the Supreme Court of Canada are designated to act in the order of their seniority on the Court. There is no specific honourific associated with the office of Administrator but the holders of the office are as much a representative of the Crown as a Governor General and generally

19. RSC 1985, App. II No. 5

20. RSC 1985, App. II, No. 31

ought to be addressed in person in the same manner as a Governor General.

The Administrator of Canada's Formal Style and Title

Administrator of Canada

The Administrator's Honourific Titles

As the Governor General of Canada is entitled to the prefix title of *Your Excellency* and honourific title of *The Right Honourable* before their name in correspondence, the same honourific should be extended to the Chief Justice of Canada when he or she is acting as the Administrator of Canada. The Chief Justice of Canada is one of only three officials of the Government of Canada who are entitled to the honourific title of *The Right Honourable*.

Where the Administrator of Canada is not the Chief Justice of Canada but rather a puisne justice of the Supreme Court of Canada, the courtesy of the prefix title of *Your Excellency* should still be extended to them while acting as the Administrator but as puisne justices of the Supreme Court are only granted the honourific title of *The Honourable*, rather than the higher title of The Right Honourable. A puisne justice acting as the Administrator of Canada should be addressed in correspondence using the title of *The Honourable*, instead of the title of The Right Honourable.

Addressing the Administrator of Canada in Person

When appearing before the Administrator of Canada, Canadians should refer to the Administrator firstly as *Your Excellency*, or *Excellency*, and thereafter as *Ma'am*, if the Administrator is a woman, or *Sir* if the Administrator is a man. The Administrator is not referred to in conversation by their title of office (i.e., they are not called Administrator in conversation)

Correspondence With the Administrator of Canada

Correspondence with the Administrator of Canada should be addressed as follows:

> (Female Chief Justice of Canada acting as the Administrator of Canada)

> Her Excellency the Right Honourable Chief Justice . . . (Insert the name and any post-nominal letters, if known[21])
> Administrator of Canada
> Rideau Hall
> 1 Sussex Drive Ottawa, Ontario
> K1A 0A1

> or

> (Male Chief Justice of Canada acting as the Administrator of Canada)

> His Excellency the Right Honourable Chief Justice . . . (Insert the name and any post-nominal letters, if known[22])
> Administrator of Canada
> Rideau Hall
> 1 Sussex Drive Ottawa, Ontario
> K1A 0A1

Where a puisne justice of the Supreme Court of Canada is acting as Administrator of Canada:

> (Female Justice of the Supreme Court of Canada acting as the Administrator of Canada)

21. A Chief Justice is invariably appointed to the Privy Council and will bear the post-nominal letters P.C.)

22. A Chief Justice is invariably appointed to the Privy Council and will bear the post-nominal letters P.C.)

Her Excellency The Honourable Justice . . . (Insert the name and any post-nominal letters, if known)
Administrator of Canada
Rideau Hall
1 Sussex Drive Ottawa, Ontario
K1A 0A1

or

(Male puisne Justice of Canada acting as the Administrator of Canada)

His Excellency The Honourable Justice . . . (Insert the name and any post-nominal letters, if known)
Administrator of Canada
Rideau Hall
1 Sussex Drive Ottawa, Ontario
K1A 0A1

The beginning salutation in a letter:

Excellency:

The closing salutation in a letter:

Yours Truly,

24. The Administrator of a Province

Section 67 of the *Constitution Act, 1867* provides a power for the Federal Ministry, acting formally in the guise of the Governor General in Council to appoint an Administrator of a Province where the Lieutenant Governor is unable to carry out the functions of their office due to absence, illness, or some other inability which can include their death in office. Since 1953 permanent Administrators have been designated and normally the Chief Justice of the Province will exercise the office of Administrator of a Province. Where a Chief Justice is unable to act as the Administrator, a puisne justice of the Provincial

Court of Appeal will normally be appointed in their stead. There is no specific honourific associated with the office of the Administrator of a Province but the holders of the office are as much a representative of the Crown as a Lieutenant Governor and generally ought to be addressed in person in the same manner as a Lieutenant Governor when acting as an Administrator.

The Administrator of a Province's Formal Style and Title

The Administrator of the Province of . . .(insert Province)

The Administrator's Honourific Titles

As the Lieutenant Governor of a Province is entitled to the prefix title of *Your Honour,* and honourific title of *The Honourable* before their name in correspondence, the same honourific should be extended to the Chief Justice of a Province or a Justice of a Provincial Court of Appeal when he or she is acting as the Administrator of their Province. (The Chief Justice of a Province and a Justice of a Provincial superiour court are entitled to the honourific title of *The Honourable* while holding judicial office.

Addressing the Administrator of a Province in Person

When appearing before the Administrator of a Province, Canadians should refer to the Administrator firstly as *Your Honour,* and thereafter as *Ma'am,* if the Administrator is a woman, or *Sir* if the Administrator is a man. The Administrator is not referred to in conversation by their title of office (i.e., they are not called Administrator in conversation)

Correspondence with the Administrator of a Province

Correspondence with the Administrator of a Province should be addressed as follows:

(Female Administrator)

Her Honour The Honourable Chief Justice/Justice . . . (Insert the name and any post-nominal letters, if known)
Administrator of (Insert the name of the Province)
mailing address (Insert the mailing address from the list of offices of the Lieutenant Governors in the appendix)

or

(Male Administrator)

His Honour the Honourable Chief Justice/Justice . . . (Insert the name and any post-nominal letters, if known)
Administrator of (Insert the name of the Province)
mailing address (Insert the mailing address from the list of offices of the Lieutenant Governors in the appendix)

The beginning salutation in a letter:

Your Honour:

or

My dear Administrator:

The closing salutation in a letter:

Yours Truly,

THE FEDERAL EXECUTIVE

The Government of Canada is the Federal Government of the country and exercises the powers specifically granted to it by the Canadian Constitution, as well as residual powers that can encompass new constitutional subjects that did not exist when the country's constitution was first created in 1867. The responsibilities of the Federal Government encompass the whole country as well as matters concerning foreign relations with other countries.

The Federal executive branch of government consists of the Ministry that is formed by the political party that has the confidence of the House of Commons, either directly through its members or with the support of the members of another party, and has been chosen by the Governor General to carry out the governance of the country in the name of the Sovereign.

25. Privy Councillors

At the Federal level, a governing ministry is formed from an elected group of members of the House of Commons, and perhaps one or two members of the appointed Senate of Canada, who are summoned to become members of the King's Privy Council for Canada. The members of the Privy Council are the confidential advisors to the Sovereign of Canada and the Governor General of Canada concerning all matters that are within the constitutional jurisdiction of the Federal Government. Privy Councillors hold office for life and assume their office by swearing an oath of allegiance to the Sovereign, and an oath to keep confidential those matters that come to their knowledge by virtue of their office.

Privy Councillor's Honourific Title

The Crown has conferred upon Privy Councillors the prefix title of *The Honourable* and the right to use the post-nominal letters of P.C. (for Privy Councillor) which they retain for so long as they remain members of the Privy Council (generally for life). Any person who is appointed as a Federal Minister is first appointed to the Privy Council if they are not already a member of the Privy Council. Thereafter, they will take their oath of office as a Minister. Where a Privy Councillor is currently a Minister they should be addressed in their capacity as a Minister of the Crown (see below under Ministers and Ministers of State). If they are not currently a Cabinet Minister they should be addressed as described below.

Addressing a Privy Councillor who is not a Minister in Person

A Privy Councillor remains an ordinary citizen and subject of the Canadian Sovereign and should be addressed in the same manner as any other Canadian would be addressed in appropriate social contexts. Depending on the circumstances, and the relationship between the speakers, a Privy Councillor may be addressed as, for example, *Mr.* Smith or *Ms.* Smith. Where the circumstances are very formal, or there is a great age disparity between the speakers, the Privy Counsellor may be addressed as *Sir* or *Ma'am*.

Correspondence With a Privy Councillor who is not a Cabinet Minister

> The Honourable ... (Insert the name and the post-nominal letters P.C., and then any other post-nominal letters, if known)
> (Insert personal address of the recipient)
>
> The beginning salutation in a letter:
>
> *Dear Sir:*
>
> or
>
> *Dear Madam:*
>
> The closing salutation in a letter:
>
> *Yours Truly,*

26. Addressing the Spouse of a Privy Councillor

There is no special form of address for the spouse of a Privy Councillor whether the Privy Councillor is holding Ministerial office or not. The spouse of a Privy Councillor is always addressed in the same manner as any other Canadian citizen.

Correspondence with the Spouse of a Privy Councillor

Correspondence with the spouse of a Privy Councillor should be framed in the same way as correspondence with any other Canadian citizen.

The Federal Ministry

The Ministry at the Federal level consists of those persons who have been summoned by the Governor General to be Privy Councillors and who have been chosen to fill the office of a Minister, or a Minister of State, by the Prime Minister and thereafter have been appointed to their designated office by the Governor General.

27. The Prime Minister

The Prime Minister is the head of the Canadian Federal Government, appointed by the Governor General of Canada based upon his or her demonstrated ability to command a majority of the votes in the House of Commons, the lower house of the Canadian Parliament. The Prime Minister is generally regarded as the most important public official in the country. The Prime Minister is one of two offices in the Federal Ministry that does not have a basis in statute law, as historically, the office was created as an exercise of the royal prerogative powers of the Crown.

The Prime Minister's Honourific Titles

A Prime Minister of Canada is entitled to the honourific title of *The Right Honourable* before their name in correspondence.

Addressing the Prime Minister in Person

When appearing before the Prime Minister of Canada in a formal setting, Canadians should refer to him or her by their title of office, i.e. they should be called *Prime Minister* in an address or conversation. Note, that a Canadian Prime Minister should not be addressed as Mr. Prime Minister, or Ms/Madam Prime Minister, as those are foreign forms of address that are not customary in Canada.

In an informal social setting, the Prime Minister may be addressed as *Mr./M./Ms./Mrs./Mme. etc, (surname)* or as *Sir*, or *Ma'am*. A Prime Minister should never be addressed by their first name unless the Prime Minister specifically invites someone to address them in that manner.

Correspondence With the Prime Minister of Canada

Correspondence with the Prime Minister of Canada should be addressed as follows:

> The Right Honourable (Insert the name, the post-nominal letters P.C., M.P., and then any other post-nominal letters, if known)
> The Office of the Prime Minister
> and Privy Council
> 80 Wellington Street
> Ottawa, Ontario
> K1P 5K9
>
> The beginning salutation in a letter:
>
> *Dear Prime Minister:*
>
> or
>
> *Prime Minister:*
>
> The closing salutation in a letter:
>
> *Yours Truly,*

28. The Spouse of a Prime Minister

The spouse of the Prime Minister is an ordinary citizen and subject of the Canadian Sovereign and they should be addressed in the same manner as other citizens should be addressed, for example, as *Mr.* Smith, or *Ms.* Smith. Where the circumstances are very formal, or there is a great age disparity between the speakers, the spouse of a Prime Minister may be addressed as *Sir* or *Ma'am*.

Correspondence with the spouse of a Prime Minister should be framed in the same way as correspondence with any other Canadian citizen. The spouse of a Prime Minister should never be addressed or referred to as the First Lady, or the First Gentleman. Those are foreign forms of address that are not customary in Canada.

29. Former Prime Ministers

A former Prime Minister retains the honourific title of *The Right Honourable* for life and should be addressed as such in correspondence.

Addressing a former Prime Minister in Person

A former Prime Minister is an ordinary citizen and subject of the Canadian Sovereign and should be addressed in the same manner as any other Canadian would be addressed in appropriate social contexts. Depending on the circumstances, and the relationship between the speakers, a former Prime Minister should be addressed as, for example, *Mr.* Smith or *Ms.* Smith. Where the circumstances are very formal, or there is a great age disparity between the speakers, the former Prime Minister may be addressed as *Sir* or *Ma'am*.

Correspondence With a Former Prime Minister of Canada

The Right Honourable . . . (Insert the name and

any post-nominal letters, if known)
(Insert personal address of the recipient)

The beginning salutation in a letter:

Dear Sir:

or

Dear Madam:

The closing salutation in a letter:

Yours Truly,

30. The Spouse of a Former Prime Minister of Canada

The spouse of a former Prime Minister is addressed in the same manner as any other Canadian citizen.

Addressing the Spouse of a Former Prime Minister of Canada in Person

They are addressed in the same manner as other citizens should be addressed, for example, as *Mr.* Smith or *Ms.* Smith. Where the circumstances are very formal, or there is a great age disparity between the speakers, the spouse of the former Prime Minister may be addressed as *Sir* or *Ma'am.*

Correspondence With the Spouse of a Former Prime Minister of Canada

Ms./Mrs./Mme./Mr./M. . . . (Insert the name and any personal post-nominal letters, if known)
(Insert the personal address of the recipient)

The beginning salutation in a letter:

Dear Madam:

or

Dear Sir:

The closing salutation in a letter:

Yours Truly,

31. The President of the King's/Queen's Privy Council for Canada

Like the office of the Prime Minister of Canada, the office of the President of the King's Privy Council for Canada (or Queen's Privy Council for Canada when a woman holds the Throne) was created by an exercise of the royal prerogative powers of the Crown at confederation in 1867 and does not have a structure in statute law. The duties of the President of the Privy Council therefore are not clearly defined and the office can be used by the Prime Minister to assign specific and unrelated functions that are important to the overall priorities of a governing Ministry. Often the office of the President of the Privy Council is combined with another ministerial office and, in the past, the office quite often was also held by the Prime Minister of the day. The current practice is not to join this office to that of the Prime Minister and most frequently (but not invariably) it is associated with the Minister of the government who is responsible for intergovernmental affairs.

Addressing the President of the King's (or Queen's) Privy Council for Canada in Person

When appearing before the President of the King's Privy Council for Canada in a formal setting, Canadians should refer to him or her by their title of office and their name, i.e. they should be called *President* in an address or conversation. Note, the President of the King's (or Queen's) Privy Council for Canada should not be addressed as Mr. or Ms/Mrs. President, as that is a foreign form of address that is not customary in Canada.

In an informal social setting, the President of the Privy Council may be addressed as *Mr./M./Ms./Mrs./Mme. (surname)*, or as *Sir,* or *Ma'am.*

Correspondence With the President of the King's Privy Council for Canada

Correspondence with the President of the King's Privy Council for Canada should be addressed as follows:

> The Honourable (Insert the name, the post-nom-inal letters P.C., M.P., and then any other post-nominal letters, if known)
> The Office of the President
> of the Privy Council
> House of Commons
> Ottawa, Ontario
> K1A 0A6

> The beginning salutation in a letter:

> *Dear President (insert the surname of the individual)*

> The closing salutation in a letter:

> *Yours Truly,*

32. Ministers without Portfolio

A Minister without Portfolio is a Minister of the Crown appointed under the royal prerogative power who is not assigned to any department or ministry of state. In the past, appointments of a Minister without Portfolio were sometimes made to ensure that a geographical balance in the Federal Ministry and Cabinet was maintained before the modern proliferation of specific government departments or agencies to which a minister could be appointed. In recent times it has been possible to address the geographic balance of the Ministry without having to appoint ministers who do not have specific duties, and consequently, the practice of appointing a Minister without Portfolio has become infrequent.

The Minister Without Portfolio's Honourific Title

A Minister Without Portfolio is entitled to the honourific title of *The Honourable* before their name in correspondence. A former Minister retains the honourific title of *The Honourable* for life, or so long as they continue to be a Privy Councillor.

Addressing the Minister Without Portfolio in Person

When appearing before a Minister Without Portfolio in a formal setting, Canadians should refer to him or her by their title of office, i.e. they should be called *Minister* in an address or conversation. Note, that a Canadian Minister should not be addressed as Mr./ Ms./Mrs. Minister, as those are foreign forms of address that are not customary in Canada.

In an informal social setting, the Minister may be addressed as *Mr./M./Ms./Mrs./Mme. (surname)* or as *Sir*, or *Ma'am*.

Correspondence With a Minister Without Portfolio

Correspondence with Minister Without Portfolio should be addressed as follows:

> The Honourable (Insert the name, the post-nominal letters P.C., M.P., and then any other postnominal letters, if known)
> House of Commons
> Ottawa, Ontario
> K1A 0A6

> The beginning salutation in a letter:

> *Dear Minister:*

> The closing salutation in a letter:

Yours Truly,

33. Minister of a Department

A departmental Minister has been placed in charge of a department of the government. Federal Ministers are appointed by the Governor General of Canada on the recommendation of the Prime Minister of Canada. Departments are established through legislation approved by Parliament. All departmental Ministers are sworn in as members of the King's Privy Council for Canada before they are appointed as Ministers. A Minister serves in office at the pleasure of the Prime Minister who appointed them and they can removed, or given other ministerial responsibilities, at the request of the Prime Minister.

The Minister's Honourific Title

A Minister is entitled to the honourific title of *The Honourable* before their name in any correspondence. A former Minister retains the honourific title of *The Honourable* for life, or so long as they continue to be a Privy Councillor.

Addressing a Minister in Person

When appearing before a Minister in a formal setting, Canadians should refer to him or her by their title of office, i.e. they should be called *Minister* in an address, or conversation. Note that a Canadian Minister should not be addressed as Mr./Ms./Mrs./Madame Minister, as those are foreign forms of address that are not customary in Canada.

In an informal social setting, the Minister may be addressed as *Mr./M./Ms./Mrs./Mme. (surname)* or as *Sir,* or *Ma'am.*

Correspondence With a Minister of a Department

Correspondence with a Minister of a Department who is a member of the House of Commons should be addressed as follows:

The Honourable . . . (Insert the surname, the post-nominal letters P.C., M.P., and then any other post-nominal letters, if known)
Minister of . . . (Insert the name of the Department, e.g. Finance)
House of Commons
Ottawa, Ontario
K1A 0A6

The beginning salutation in a letter:

Dear Minister:

The closing salutation in a letter:

Yours Truly,

If the Minister is a member of the Senate of Canada they should be addressed as follows:

Senator the Honourable . . . (Insert the surname and the post-nominal letters P.C., and then any other post-nominal letters, if known)
Minister of . . . (Insert the name of the Department, e.g. Finance)
The Senate of Canada
Ottawa, Ontario
K1A 0A4

The beginning salutation in a letter:

Dear Minister:

The closing salutation in a letter:

Yours Truly,

34. Associate Ministers of a Department

Some departmental statutes, such as the *Department of National*

Defence Act[23], provide for the appointment of an Associate Minister. Such Ministers are given departmental responsibilities and are a means of reducing the ministerial workload in very heavy portfolios. An Associate Minister is in the same position as the Minister of the Department for all protocol purposes and should be addressed and corresponded with in the same manner as described above for a departmental minister, with the exception that their title is *"Associate Minister of . . ."*.

35. Ministers of State

A Minister of State is a person who is appointed to hold office under the *Ministries and Ministers of State Act*[24]. This is a type of junior Minister in the Canadian Federal Government and there are two types of Ministers of State. A Minister of State can be appointed where there is a need for a policy issue to be addressed and developed by the Federal Government. For this purpose, a Minister of State may be appointed and a portion of the Public Service of Canada may be established to support the work of the Minister of State. The second type of Minister of State is a Minister of State assigned to assist the Minister of a Department in the work of that department. In such cases, a separate portion of the Public Service of Canada is not established to support the work of the Minister of State. Rather, the Minister of State works within an existing department, in conjunction with the Minister of the Department in which they both serve.

The Minister of State's Honourific Title

A Minister of State is entitled to the honourific title of *The Honourable* before their name in correspondence. A former Minister of State retains the honourific title of *The Honourable* for life, or so long as they continue to be a Privy Councillor.

---

23. RSC 1985, c. N-5, s. 6
24. RSC 1985, c. M-8

Addressing a Minister of State in Person

When appearing before a Minister of State in a formal setting, Canadians should refer to him or her by their title of office, i.e. they should be called *Minister* in an address or conversation. Note that a Canadian Minister of State should not be addressed as Mr./ Ms./Mrs./Madame Minister, as those are foreign forms of address that are not customary in Canada.

In an informal social setting, the Minister of State may be addressed as *Mr./M./Ms./Mrs./Mme. (surname)*, or as *Sir*, or *Ma'am*.

Correspondence With a Minister of State

Correspondence with a Minister of State who is a member of the House of Commons should be addressed as follows:

> The Honourable . . . (Insert the full name and post-nominal letters P.C., M.P.[25]
> Minister of State (for) . . . (Insert the name of the Ministry of State or the name of the portfolio assignment held by the Minister of State[26])
> House of Commons
> Ottawa, Ontario
> K1A 0A6
>
> The beginning salutation in a letter:
>
> *Dear Minister:*
>
> The closing salutation in a letter:
>
> *Yours Truly,*

---

25. Omit M.P. if the Minister of State is a Senator.

26. For example, the Minister of Digital Government.

If a Minister of State is a member of the Senate of Canada they should be addressed as follows:

> Senator the Honourable . . . (Insert the name and the post-nominal letters P.C., and then any other post-nominal letters, if known)
> Minister of State (for) . . . (Insert the name of the Ministry of State or the name of the portfolio assignment held by the Minister of State[27])
> The Senate of Canada
> Ottawa, Ontario
> K1A 0A4

> The beginning salutation in a letter:

> *Dear Minister:*

> The closing salutation in a letter:

> *Yours Truly,*

36. Territorial Commissioners

Canada's three territories, Yukon, Northwest Territories, and Nunavut occupy a vast portion of Canadian geography but they have a subordinate status in comparison to the provinces of Canada. Constitutionally, they remain as Federal territories, although they have been given extensive control over local matters by agreement with the Federal government. Unlike a province, there is no official representative of the King at the head of the territorial governments (as constitutionally the Governor General fulfils that function). Rather, another official, the Commissioner of a Territory, represents the Minister of Northern Affairs and carries out, as a Federal Officer, similar responsibilities to those performed by a Lieutenant Governor of a Province.

---

27. For example, the Minister of Digital Government.

A Commissioner's Honourific Title

A Commissioner of a Canadian territory is entitled to the honourific title of *The Honourable* before their name in correspondence. A Territorial Commissioner retains their honourific title only while they hold office.

Addressing the Commissioner of a Territory in Person

When appearing before a Commissioner of a territory of Canada, Canadians should refer to the Commissioner firstly by their title of office (i.e., as *Commissioner* or *Commissioner (insert last name)* or they may be referred to by their common honourific and surname (e.g. *Mr./M./Ms./Mrs./Mme. (insert last name)*. Subsequently, they may be addressed as *Madam*, if the Commissioner is a woman, or *Sir* if the Commissioner is a man. In an informal social setting, the Commissioner may be addressed as *Mr./M./Ms./Mrs./Mme. (surname)*, or as *Sir* or *Madam*. A Commissioner should never be addressed by their first name unless the Commissioner specifically invites someone to address them in that manner.

Correspondence with a Commissioner of a Territory

Correspondence with a territorial Commissioner should be addressed as follows:

> The Honourable . . . (Insert full name and any post-nominal letters, if known)
> Commissioner of . . . (Insert the name of the Territory)
> mailing address (Insert the mailing address from the list of addresses in the appendix)

> The beginning salutation in a letter:

> *Dear Commissioner:*

> or

My dear Commissioner:

The closing salutation in a letter:

Yours Truly,

37. Deputy Commissioners

Provision is made in the constitutional instruments of two of the northern territories for the appointment of a Deputy Commissioner. In the Northwest Territories and Nunavut whenever the territorial Commissioner is unable to carry out their duties or they are absent from the territory a Deputy Commissioner may act on their behalf. The Deputy Commissioner of a territory when acting on behalf of a Commissioner of a territory does so as an alternate of the Commissioner, and not as a subordinate officer.

In the Yukon Territory the office of Deputy Commissioner does not exist and whenever the Commissioner of Yukon Territory is not present in the territory or is present but unable to carry out their duties, or the office is vacant the territorial constitution provides for the appointment of a judge of the Supreme Court of the Territory to fulfil the functions of the Commissioner.

A Deputy Commissioner's Honourific Title

A Deputy Commissioner of a Canadian territory has no special honourific title.

Addressing the Deputy Commissioner of a Territory in Person

When appearing before a Deputy Commissioner of a territory of Canada, Canadians should refer to the Deputy Commissioner by their title of office (i.e., as *Deputy Commissioner*, or *Deputy Commissioner (insert last name)*, or they may be referred to by a common honourific and their surname (e.g.

Mr./M./Mrs./Ms./Mme. (insert last name). A Deputy Commissioner of a Territory should never be addressed by their first name unless the Deputy Commissioner specifically invites someone to address them in that manner.

Correspondence with a Deputy Commissioner of a Territory

Correspondence with a territorial Deputy Commissioner should be addressed as follows:

> Mr./M./Ms./Mrs./Mme. (Insert full name and any post-nominal letters, if known)
> Deputy Commissioner of . . . (Insert the name of the Territory)
> mailing address (Insert the mailing address from the list of addresses in the appendix)

> The beginning salutation in a letter:

> *Dear Deputy Commissioner:*

> or

> *My dear Deputy Commissioner:*

> The closing salutation in a letter:

> *Yours Truly,*

38. The Administrator of a Territory

In the Northwest Territories or Nunavut in situations where a Commissioner of a Territory or a Deputy Commissioner of a Territory is not present within the territory or is present but unable to carry out their duties, or the office is vacant, the territorial constitutions provide for the appointment of a judge of the Supreme Court of the Territory to fulfil the functions of the Commissioner as Administrator of the territory.

In Yukon, where there is no Deputy Commissioner, the territorial constitution requires that in the absence of, or inability of the Commissioner to Act, or where the office of Commissioner is vacant, a judge of the Supreme Court of Yukon will act as the Administrator of the territory.

As in the case of a Deputy Commissioner of a territory, in territories where that office exists, the Administrator of a territory acts as an alternate to the Commissioner and is not an assistant to the Commissioner, or in any way subordinate to the Commissioner.

The Administrator's Honourific Titles

As the Justice of a Superior Court is entitled to the prefix title of *Your Honour*, and honourific title of *The Honourable* before their name in correspondence, the same honourific should be extended to them when he or she is acting as the Administrator of their Territory.

Addressing the Administrator of a Territory in Person

When appearing before the Administrator of a Territory, Canadians should refer to the Administrator firstly as *Your Honour*, and thereafter as *Madam*, if the Administrator is a woman, or *Sir* if the Administrator is a man. The Administrator is not referred to in conversation by their title of office (i.e., they are not called Administrator in conversation)

Correspondence with the Administrator of a Territory

Correspondence with the Administrator of a Territory should be addressed as follows:

> (Female Administrator)

> The Honourable Chief Justice/Justice . . . (Insert surname and any post-nominal letters, if known) Administrator of (Insert the name of the Terri-

tory)
mailing address (Insert the mailing address from the list of offices of the Territorial Commissioners in the appendix)

or

(Male Administrator)

The Honourable Chief Justice/Justice . . . (Insert surname and any post-nominal letters, if known) Administrator of (Insert the name of the Territory)
mailing address (Insert the mailing address from the list of offices of the Territorial Commissioners in the appendix)

The beginning salutation in a letter:

Your Honour:

or

My dear Administrator:

The closing salutation in a letter:

Yours Truly,

THE PARLIAMENT OF CANADA

39. The Speaker of the Senate

The Speaker of the Senate of Canada is the presiding officer of the upper house of the Parliament of Canada. He or she enforces the rules for the conduct of proceedings within the Senate Chamber and carries out administrative functions concerning the Senate. The Speaker is appointed by the Governor General from amongst the members of the Senate upon the recommendation of the Prime Minister.

The Honourific Title of the Speaker of the Senate

As a member of the Senate, the Speaker is entitled to the honourific title of *The Honourable* before their name in any correspondence. A former Speaker retains the honourific title of *The Honourable* for life.

Addressing the Speaker of the Senate in Person

When appearing before the Speaker of the Senate of Canada, Canadians should refer to them as *Madam Speaker* if the Speaker is a woman or *Mr. Speaker* if the incumbent is a man.

In an informal social setting, the Speaker of the Senate may be addressed as *Mr./M./Ms./Mrs./Mme. (surname)*, or as *Sir* or *Madam*. The Speaker of the Senate should never be addressed by their first name unless the Speaker specifically invites someone to address them in that manner.

Correspondence with the Speaker of the Senate

Correspondence with the Speaker of the Senate should be addressed as follows:

> The Honourable Senator . . . (Insert full name and any post-nominal letters)
> Speaker of the Senate
> The Senate
> Ottawa, Ontario
> K1A 0A4

> The beginning salutation in a letter:

> *Dear Mr. Speaker:*

> or

> *Dear Madam Speaker:*

> The closing salutation in a letter:

Yours Truly,

40. The Speaker of the House of Commons

The Speaker of the House of Commons is the presiding officer of the lower house of the Parliament of Canada. He or she enforces the rules for the conduct of proceedings and adjudicates disputes over parliamentary procedure within the Chamber of the House of Commons. The Speaker of the House of Commons also carries out administrative functions concerning the Commons. The Speaker is elected by the members of the House of Commons.

The Honourific Title of the Speaker of the House of Commons

The Speaker of the House of Commons is entitled to the honourific title of *The Honourable* before their name in any correspondence, while they hold the office of Speaker of the House of Commons. However, it is a not uncommon practice for the Speaker of the House of Commons to also be summoned to be a member of the King's Privy Council for Canada and in such cases, a Speaker of the House of Commons who is a Privy Councillor will be entitled to retain the prefix of *The Honourable* for life (as well as the post-nominal letters P.C.). All members of the House of Commons, including the Speaker, are entitled to the post-nominal letters M.P. (standing for Member of Parliament) while they are a member of the House of Commons.

Addressing the Speaker of the House of Commons in Person

When appearing before the Speaker of the House of Commons of Canada, Canadians should refer to them as *Madam Speaker*, if the Speaker is a woman or *Mr. Speaker*, if the incumbent is a man.

In an informal social setting, the Speaker of the House of Commons may be addressed as *Mr./M./Ms./Mrs./Mme. (surname)*, or as *Sir* or *Madam*. The Speaker of the House of Commons should never be addressed by their first name unless the Speaker specifically invites someone to address them in that manner.

Correspondence with the Speaker of the House of Commons

Correspondence with the Speaker of the House of Commons should be addressed as follows:

> The Honourable (Insert full name) M.P. (Insert any other post-nominal letters, if known)
> Speaker of the House of Commons
> House of Commons
> Ottawa, Ontario
> K1A 0A6

> The beginning salutation in a letter:

> *Dear Mr. Speaker:*

> or

> *Dear Madam Speaker:*

> The closing salutation in a letter:

> *Yours Truly,*

41. Senators

Senators are members of the upper house of the Parliament of Canada. They are appointed by the Governor General on the recommendation of the Prime Minister and they hold office until their seventy-fifth birthday.

The Honourific Title of a Senator

A member of the Senate is entitled to the honourific title of *The Honourable* before their name in any correspondence. A Senator who has been appointed to the Ministry will also be summoned to the Privy Council and will therefore also bear the post-nominal letters P.C.

A former Senator retains the honourific title of *The Honourable* for life.

Addressing a Senator in Person

A Senator should be addressed in conversation by their title of office (i.e., as *Senator . . . (insert last name)*.

In an informal social setting, a Senator may be addressed as *Mr./M./Ms./Mrs./Mme. (surname)*, or as *Sir* or *Madam*. A Senator should never be addressed by their first name unless the Senator specifically invites someone to address them in that manner.

Correspondence with a Senator

Correspondence with a Senator should be addressed as follows:

> The Honourable Senator . . . (Insert full name and any post-nominal letters, if known)
> The Senate
> Ottawa, Ontario
> K1A 0A4

> The beginning salutation in a letter:

> *Dear Senator:*

> The closing salutation in a letter:

> *Yours Truly,*

42. Parliamentary Secretaries

A Parliamentary Secretary is a member of Parliament within the Parliamentary caucus of the governing political party who has been appointed by the Prime Minister of Canada to assist a Minister, or a Minister of State, with routine parliamentary matters. The duties normally handled by a Parliamentary Secretary are in the nature of liaison duties between the Minister and the members of the caucus of the governing party. They may also handle routine parliamentary matters in the chamber and attend parliamentary committees in a non-voting capacity.

The Honourific Title of a Parliamentary Secretary

A Parliamentary Secretary does not possess an honourific title. As a member of the House of Commons, they are entitled to the post-nominal letters M.P. denoting a Member of Parliament.

Addressing a Parliamentary Secretary in Person

A Parliamentary Secretary may be addressed as *Mr./M./Ms./Mrs./Mme. (surname)*, or as *Sir* or *Ma'am*. A Parliamentary Secretary should never be addressed by their first name unless the Parliamentary Secretary specifically invites someone to address them in that manner.

Correspondence with a Parliamentary Secretary

Correspondence with a Parliamentary Secretary should be addressed as follows:

> Mr./M./Ms./Mrs./Mme. (Insert full name) M.P.
> (Insert other known post-nominals)
> House of Commons
> Ottawa, Ontario
> K1A 0A6

> The beginning salutation in a letter:

> *Dear Sir:*

> or

> *Dear Madam*

The closing salutation in a letter:

Yours Truly,

43. Members of Parliament

A Member of Parliament is a person who has been elected to serve in the House of Commons, the lower house of the Parliament of Canada.

The Honourific Title of a Member of Parliament

A Member of Parliament does not possess a prefix honourific title. As a member of the House of Commons, they are entitled to the use of the post-nominal letters M.P. which denotes a Member of Parliament.

Addressing a Member of Parliament in Person

A Member of Parliament should be addressed in conversation as *Mr./M./Ms./Mrs./Mme. (surname)*, or as *Sir* or *Ma'am*. A Member of Parliament should never be addressed by their first name unless the Member of Parliament specifically invites someone to address them in that manner.

Correspondence with a Member of Parliament

Correspondence with a Member of Parliament should be addressed as follows:

> Mr./M./Ms./Mrs./Mme. (Insert full name) M.P.
> (Insert other known post-nominals)[28]
> House of Commons
> Ottawa, Ontario
> K1A 0A6

---

28. Note that where a Member of Parliament is also a Privy Councillor, the prefix title of *The Honourable* should be inserted before their name in correspondence and the post-nominal letters P.C. should precede the letters M.P.

The beginning salutation in a letter:

Dear Sir:

or

Dear Madam

The closing salutation in a letter:

Yours Truly,

Addressing Parliamentary Officials

Officials of the Parliament of Canada are considered to be procedural officers serving all parliamentarians in a neutral and non-partisan fashion.

44. Clerk of the Senate and Clerk of the Parliaments

The Clerk of the Senate and Clerk of the Parliaments occupies a dual office. As Clerk of the Senate, he or she is the senior administrative official in the Senate Administration. The Clerk of the Senate supports the Senate's legislative process, and advises the Speaker of the Senate on matters of parliamentary procedure.

As Clerk of the Parliaments the incumbent is the custodian of all statutes passed by the House of Commons and Senate and given royal assent. The Clerk of the Parliaments certifies the authenticity of any true copy of a statute enacted by Parliament.

The Clerk of the Senate and Clerk of the Parliaments supports the legislative process of the Senate as the Chief Legislative Services Officer in the Senate and administers the legislative services section of the Senate.

45. The Usher of the Black Rod

The Usher of the Black Rod is a senior officer of ancient origins in the British Parliamentary system. The office began as one within the Royal Household and later became a Parliamentary Messenger. The position is politically neutral, as the Black Rod acts as the King's Messenger, and the personal attendant of the Sovereign and the Governor General when they are present in Parliament. The Black Rod also has important responsibilities for Parliamentary protocol.

The name of the office reflects the black cane that is carried by the incumbent as a symbol of their authority. For many centuries in Britain as well as in post-confederation Canada the office was styled as The Gentleman Usher of the Black Rod but in 1997, upon the appointment of the first female person as the Usher, the title and style was altered to remove the reference to gender and the office is now titled as The Usher of the Black Rod[29]. The Black Rod, as the Usher is commonly known within the parliamentary precinct, is appointed by the Governor General on the advice of the Prime Minister.

46. Law Clerk and Parliamentary Counsel

The Law Clerk and Parliamentary Counsel provides politically non-partisan advice on all legal questions arising within the Senate or its committees and advises the Speaker of the Senate when required. The Law Clerk also provides legal advice to Senators with respect to their public duties and assists Senators with legislative drafting matters.

47. Clerk of the House of Commons

The Clerk of the House of Commons is a non-partisan procedural officer who assists the Speaker and members of the House of Commons concerning parliamentary procedures and precedents and maintains the records of the House of Commons. He or she is the chief administrative officer of the House of Commons and acts as the Secretary of the Board of Internal

29. Senate Journals, November 6, 1997

Economy which is responsible for the administration of the House of Commons

Addressing the Procedural Officers of the Parliament in Person

A Procedural Officer of the Parliament should be addressed in conversation as *Mr./M./Ms./Mrs./Mme. (surname)*, or as *Sir* or *Ma'am*. A Procedural Officer of Parliament should never be addressed by their first name unless they specifically invite someone to address them in that manner.

Correspondence with a Procedural Officer of the Parliament

Correspondence with a Procedural Officer of the Parliament should be addressed as follows:

> Mr./M./Mrs/Ms/Mme. (Insert full name and any post-nominal letters, if known)
> (Title) . . . (Insert the full title of the Office held by the recipient)
> Senate of Canada
> 2 Rideau St, Ottawa, ON
> K1A 0A4

> or

> Mr.M.//Mrs/Ms/Mme. (Insert full name and any post-nominal letters, if known)
> (Title) . . . (Insert the full title of the Office held by the recipient)
> House of Commons
> Ottawa, Ontario
> Canada
> K1A 0A6

The beginning salutation in a letter:

Dear Sir:

or

Dear Madam

The closing salutation in a letter:

Yours Truly,

48. Dominion Offices

At Confederation in 1867, the principal father of Confederation, John A. Macdonald, wanted to describe the new confederation formally as the Kingdom of Canada. However, the Foreign Office in London recoiled from that suggestion because of a concern that the United States would be unduly sensitive to the formal proclamation of a new monarchical state in North America.[30]

As a compromise between Macdonald's desire to promote the monarchical nature of the country and the desire of the Foreign Office to be wary of inflaming American popular opinion, Sir Leonard Tilley, one of the fathers of confederation suggested that the new country be described as the Dominion of Canada. His suggestion was said to have been inspired by a biblical verse; Psalm 72:8: "He shall have dominion also from sea to sea, and from the river unto the ends of the earth." However, Great Britain had also previously used the word dominion to describe some of its overseas colonies (including, for example, Virginia) so the name Dominion of Canada was not necessarily an innovation. Over time, as the British Empire transformed into the present-day Commonwealth of Nations the word dominion came to be seen as a subordinate status reflecting a state that

---

30. The state assembly in Maine protested the monarchical designation of the new country and statements were made in the Congress but no diplomatic representations were made to Britain by the United States (Desmond Morton, *The Kingdom of Canada*, McClelland & Stewart, Toronto, 1972 at p. 324.

was almost but not quite independent. Although the name Dominion of Canada remained in use as late as the 1960's it rapidly fell into disuse in the post-war era as Canada forged its own state symbolism. Today, the name Dominion of Canada is considered to be obsolete. The country is simply described as Canada.

Nevertheless, for many years the descriptive term Dominion was employed to describe many Canadian offices and institutions. Over the past half-century, this terminology has been redacted and most references to a Dominion office have been eliminated. However, in 2024 at least two such offices remain extant, the Dominion Sculptor and the Dominion Carillonneur, both of whom are minor parliamentary officials. Dominion officials should be addressed both in person and in correspondence in the same manner as members of the Federal Public Service (*infra*, see below under Public Services).

THE PROVINCIAL EXECUTIVE

49. Executive Councillors

A person who is to be assigned to the office of a Minister of a Provincial Government is first appointed to the Executive Council of the Province, an institution that functions much like the Privy Council of Canada at the federal level. The difference between the Executive Council of a Province and the Privy Council is that the Executive Council is not a permanent constitutional body and its membership will at all times be coterminous with the membership of the Ministry of the Province for the time being that has been appointed to office by the Lieutenant Governor of each province. Members of an Executive Council of a province are entitled to be addressed in correspondence by the honourific description of *The Honourable* while they serve in office.

In the past Executive Councillors of a province did not bear any post-nominal letters while they served in office, or afterwards. However, that is changing as some provinces now permit their Executive Councillors to bear post-nominal letters to distinguish themselves as members, or former members, of a provincial Executive Council. In the Province of Nova Scotia, legislation now provides that members of the Executive Council of Nova Scotia may bear the post-nominal letters E.C.N.S. (Executive Councillor of Nova Scotia) and all former Ministers of the Crown in Nova Scotia become Honourary members of the Executive Council after their retirement and may continue to use both the post-nominal letters E.C.N.S. and the honourific *The Honourable* before their name. The same result occurs in Alberta where, as a result of legislation members of the Executive Council of Alberta may bear the post-nominal letters E.C.A. (Executive Councillor of Alberta) and all former Ministers of the Crown in Alberta become Honourary members of the Executive Council after their retirement and may continue to use both the post-nominal letters E.C.A. and the honourific *The Honourable* before their name for life.

50. The Premier

Formally, the Premier of a province is the President of the Executive Council of the Province but the expression Premier is used by custom to denote their position as the leader of the Ministry under the Provincial Crown and to differentiate their office from the Office of the Prime Minister of Canada. The addition of the province of appointment is necessary to distinguish one provincial leader from another.

It should be noted that in French the word "premier" is not available for use as a synonym for the head of the provincial government. Rather, in French the head of any provincial government is described as the "premier ministre" or Prime Minister.

A Provincial Premier is entitled to use the honourific title of *The Honourable* before their name in correspondence while in office, unless in respect of Nova Scotia or Alberta where the honourific title has been conferred on former Premiers of those provinces for life.

Addressing a Premier in Person

When appearing before a Premier of a Province in a formal setting, Canadians should refer to him or her by their title of office, i.e. they should be called *Premier* in an address or conversation[31]. Note that a Canadian Premier should not be addressed as Mr./ Ms./Mrs./Mme. Premier, as those are foreign forms of address that are not customary in Canada.

In an informal social setting, the Premier may be addressed as *Mr./M./Ms./Mrs./Mme. (surname)*, or as *Sir*, or *Madam* or *Ma'am*. A Premier should never be addressed by their first name unless the Premier specifically invites someone to address them in that manner.

Correspondence With a Premier[32]

Correspondence with a Premier who is a member of a Provincial Legislature should be addressed as follows:

> The Honourable . . . (Insert the full name and the appropriate official post-nominal letters (e.g., E.C.N.S.[33]/ E.C.A.[34] M.L.A.[35] etc., and then any

31. premier ministre in Quebec

32. Applicable only to correspondence with the Premier of Newfoundland and Labrador, Prince Edward Island, Nova Scotia, New Brunswick, Ontario, Manitoba, Saskatchewan, Alberta and British Columbia.

33. These post-nominal letters are only used in Nova Scotia

34. These post-nominal letters are only used in Alberta

35. The abbreviation M.L.A. stands for Member of the Legislative Assembly and that abbreviation is appropriate for any elected member of the legislatures of Nova Scotia, Prince Edward Island, New Brunswick, Manitoba, Saskatchewan, Alberta and British Columbia. In Newfoundland and Labrador, the correct designation is M.H.A. which stands for Member of the House of Assembly. In Quebec, the correct designation is M.N.A. which stands for

other personal post-nominal letters, if known)
Premier of the Province of _____
(Insert address of the Provincial Legislature)

The beginning salutation in a letter:

Dear Premier:

The closing salutation in a letter:

Yours Truly,

Correspondence with the Premier of Quebec

M. or Mme. (Insert the full name and the official post-nominal letters M.N.A. and then any other personal post-nominal letters, if known)[36]
premier ministre du Québec[37]
(Insert the address of the Assemblée nationale du Québec)

The beginning salutation in(an English) letter:

Dear premier ministre:

The closing salutation in (an English) letter:

Member of the National Assembly. In Ontario, the correct designation is M.P.P. which stands for Member of the Provincial Parliament. Note, however, that if a Premier is not a member of a legislature the official post-nominal letters should not be included in the address.

36. The honourific title "Honourable" is not used by a Premier or a Minister of the Government of Quebec.

37. In the French language the expression "Premier" does not exist and thus it is preferable to refer to the Premier of Quebec by his or her title in the French language, "premier ministre" in correspondence addressed to him or her. However, in a more general context in English, it is not inappropriate to describe the head of the Quebec government as the Premier of Quebec. The use of the word "Premier" in English serves to differentiate a provincial head of government from the Prime Minister, who is the head of the federal government.

Yours Truly,

51. The Spouse of a Premier

The spouse of a former Premier is addressed in the same manner as any other Canadian citizen.

Addressing the Spouse of a Premier in Person

The spouse of a former Premier is addressed in the same manner as other citizens should be addressed, for example, as *Mr.* Smith, or *Ms.* Smith. Where the circumstances are very formal, or there is a great age disparity between the speakers, the spouse of a Provincial Premier may be addressed as *Sir* or *Ma'am.*

Correspondence With the Spouse of a Premier

Ms./Mrs./Mme./Mr./M. . . . (Insert the name and any personal post-nominal letters, if known)
(Insert the personal address of the recipient)

The beginning salutation in a letter:

Dear Madam:

or

Dear Sir:

The closing salutation in a letter:

Yours Truly,

52. Former Premiers

Generally, a former Premier does not retain the honourific title of *The Honourable* once they cease to hold office unless in respect of Nova Scotia or Alberta where the honourific title has been conferred on former Premiers of those provinces for life.

Addressing a former Premier in Person

A former Premier is an ordinary citizen and subject of the Canadian Sovereign and should be addressed in the same manner as any other Canadian would be addressed in appropriate social contexts. Depending on the circumstances, and the relationship between the speakers, a former Premier should be addressed as, for example, *Mr.* Smith or *Ms.* Smith. Where the circumstances are very formal, or there is a great age disparity between the speakers, the former Premier may be addressed as *Sir* or *Ma'am*.

Correspondence With a Former Premier of a Province

1. Alberta

> The Honourable . . . (insert full name) E.C.A.
> (Insert any personal post-nominal letters, if known)
> (Insert personal address of the recipient)

2. Nova Scotia

> The Honourable . . . (insert full name) E.C.N.S.
> (Insert any personal post-nominal letters, if known)
> (Insert personal address of the recipient)

3 Newfoundland and Labrador, Prince Edward Island, New Brunswick, Quebec, Ontario, Manitoba, Saskatchewan, British Columbia:

> Mr. M. Ms., Mme, Mrs. . . . (Insert full name any post-nominal letters if known)

> The beginning salutation in a letter:

> *Dear Sir:*

or

Dear Madam:

<u>The closing salutation in a letter:</u>

Yours Truly,

53. The Spouse of a Former Premier of a Province

The spouse of a former Premier is addressed in the same manner as any other Canadian citizen.

Addressing the Spouse of a Former Premier of a Province in Person

The spouse of a former Premier is addressed in the same manner as other citizens should be addressed, for example, as *Mr.* Smith, or *Ms.* Smith. Where the circumstances are very formal, or there is a great age disparity between the speakers, the spouse of the former Provincial Premier may be addressed as *Sir* or *Ma'am.*

Correspondence With the Spouse of a Former Premier of a Province

Ms./Mrs./Mr. . . . (Insert the name and any personal post-nominal letters, if known)
(Insert the personal address of the recipient)

<u>The beginning salutation in a letter:</u>

Dear Madam:

or

Dear Sir:

<u>The closing salutation in a letter:</u>

Yours Truly,

54. Provincial Ministers

A Provincial Minister is entitled to use the honourific title of *The Honourable* before their name in correspondence while in office, unless in respect of Nova Scotia or Alberta where the honourific title shall be conferred on former Ministers of those provinces for life. The honourific title is not used in Quebec for either serving or former Ministers of the Provincial government.

Addressing a Provincial Minister in Person

When appearing before a Minister of a Province in a formal setting, Canadians should refer to him or her by their title of office, i.e. they should be called *Minister* in an address or conversation. Note that a provincial Minister should not be addressed in English as Mr./ Ms./Mrs./Madame Minister, as those are foreign forms of address that are not customary in Canada.

In an informal social setting, a Minister may be addressed as *Mr./Ms./Mrs./Mme. (surname)* or as *Sir*, or *Ma'am*. A Minister should never be addressed by their first name unless the Minister specifically invites someone to address them in that manner.

Correspondence With a Provincial Minister[38]

Correspondence with a Minister who is a member of a Provincial Legislature should be addressed as follows:

> The Honourable . . . (Insert the full name and the appropriate official post-nominal letters (e.g.,

---

38. Applicable only to correspondence with a provincial Minister in Newfoundland and Labrador, Prince Edward Island, Nova Scotia, New Brunswick, Ontario, Manitoba, Saskatchewan, Alberta and British Columbia.

E.C.N.S.[39], E.C.A.[40], M.LA.[41] etc., and then any other personal post-nominal letters, if known)
Minister of _____
Province of _____
(Insert address of the Provincial Legislature)

The beginning salutation in a letter:

Dear Minister:

The closing salutation in a letter:

Yours Truly,

Correspondence with a Minister of the Province of Quebec

M. or Mme. (Insert the full name and the official post-nominal letters M.N.A.[42] and then any other personal post-nominal letters, if known)[43]
insert Ministerial title
(Insert the address of the Assemblée nationale du Québec)

55. Former Provincial Ministers

39. These post-nominal letters are only used in Nova Scotia.
40. These post-nominal letters are only used in Alberta.
41. The abbreviation M.L.A. stands for Member of the Legislative Assembly and that abbreviation is appropriate for any elected member of the legislatures of Nova Scotia, Prince Edward Island, New Brunswick, Manitoba, Saskatchewan, Alberta and British Columbia. In Newfoundland and Labrador, the correct designation is M.H.A. which stands for Member of the House of Assembly. In Quebec, the correct designation is M.N.A. which stands for Member of the National Assembly. In Ontario, the correct designation is M.P.P. which stands for Member of the Provincial Parliament. Note, however, that if a provincial Minister is not a member of a legislature the official post-nominal letters should not be included in the address.
42. These post-nominal letters are only used in Quebec.
43. The honourific title "Honourable" is not used by a Minister of the Government of Quebec.

A former provincial Minister does not retain the honourific title of Honourable once they cease to hold office unless in respect of Nova Scotia or Alberta, where the honourific title has been conferred on former Ministers of those provinces for life Therefore only former Nova Scotia or Alberta Ministers should be addressed with the honourific title of The Honourable in correspondence.

Addressing a former Provincial Minister in Person

A former provincial Minister is an ordinary citizen and subject of the Canadian Sovereign and should be addressed in the same manner as any other Canadian would be addressed in appropriate social contexts. Depending on the circumstances, and the relationship between the speakers, a former provincial Minister should be addressed as, for example, *Mr.* Smith or *Ms.* Smith. Where the circumstances are very formal, or there is a great age disparity between the speakers, the former provincial Minister may be addressed as *Sir* or *Ma'am*.

Correspondence With a Former Minister of a Province

1. Alberta

> The Honourable . . .(insert name) E.C.A. (Insert any personal post-nominal letters, if known) (Insert personal address of the recipient)

2. Nova Scotia

> The Honourable . . .(insert name) E.C.N.S. (Insert any personal post-nominal letters, if known) (Insert personal address of the recipient)

3 Newfoundland and Labrador, Prince Edward Island, New Brunswick, Quebec, Ontario, Manitoba, Saskatchewan, British Columbia:

Mr./ M./ Ms./, Mme,/ Mrs. (Insert name and any personal post-nominal letters, if known)

The beginning salutation in a letter:

Dear Sir:

or

Dear Madam:

The closing salutation in a letter:

Yours Truly,

THE PROVINCIAL LEGISLATURES

56. The Speaker of a Provincial Legislature

The Speaker of a Provincial Legislature is the presiding officer of the assembly. He or she enforces the rules for the conduct of proceedings and adjudicates disputes over parliamentary procedure within the Chamber of the Legislatures. The Speaker also carries out administrative functions concerning the legislature. The Speaker is elected by the members of the legislature.

Addressing the Speaker of a Provincial Legislature in Person

When appearing before the Speaker of a Provincial Legislature, Canadians should refer to them as *Madam Speaker*, if the Speaker is a woman or *Mr. Speaker,* if the incumbent is a man. In the Province of Quebec, the title of the chief procedural officer of the provincial legislature is President of the National Assembly. Therefore, the incumbent should be addressed as *Madame la presidente* or *Monsieur le president.*

In an informal social setting, a Speaker of a provincial legislature may be addressed as *Mr./M./Ms./Mrs./Mme (surname)*, or as *Sir*, or *Madam.* A Speaker of a Provincial Legislature should never be addressed by their first name unless the Speaker specifically invites someone to address them in that manner.

Correspondence with the Speaker of a Provincial Legislature

Correspondence with the Speaker of a Provincial Legislature should be addressed as follows:

> The Honourable (Insert full name) (Insert post-nominal letters)
> Speaker of the _____
> (Insert provincial capital city and province
> (Insert address for the applicable provincial legislature)

> The beginning salutation in a letter:

> *Dear Mr. Speaker:*

> or

> *Dear Madam Speaker:*

> The closing salutation in a letter:

> *Yours Truly,*

Correspondence with the President of the National Assembly in the Province of Quebec

> M. or Mme. (Insert the full name and the official post-nominal letters M.N.A. and then any other personal post-nominal letters, if known)
> insert title: la presidente (if female) or le president (if male)
> (Insert the address of the Assemblée nationale du Québec)

> The beginning salutation in an (English) letter:

Dear Monsieur (insert surname)

or

Dear Madame (insert surname):

The closing salutation in an (English) letter:

Yours Truly,

57. Members of a Provincial Legislature

When appearing before a Member of a Legislature of a Province in a formal or informal setting, Canadians should refer to him or her as *Mr./ M./Ms./Mrs./Mme (surname)* or as *Sir*, or *Ma'am* unless invited to address the Member informally.

Correspondence With a Member of a Provincial Legislature

Correspondence with a member of a Provincial Legislature should be addressed as follows:

> Mr./M./ Ms./ Mrs./Mme. (Insert the full name and the appropriate official post-nominal letters (e.g., M.LA. etc., and then any other personal post-nominal letters, if known)
> (Insert address of the Provincial Legislature)

The beginning salutation in a letter:

Dear Sir:

or

Dear Madam:

The closing salutation in a letter:

Yours Truly,

THE TERRITORIAL EXECUTIVE

Canada's three territories in the north (Yukon, Northwest Territories, and Nunavut) have not yet evolved into provinces and are constitutionally subject to the federal government although in practice they operate autonomously from the federal government and, for most purposes, operate much like a provincial government, albeit on a smaller scale. Consequently, the forms of address appropriate for provincial officers are also generally applicable to their territorial counterparts.

58. The Premier

The Premier of a territory is the leader of the Territorial Ministry. A territorial Premier is entitled to use the honourific title of *The Honourable* before their name in correspondence while in office.

Addressing a Territorial Premier in Person

When appearing before a Premier of a Territory in a formal setting, Canadians should refer to him or her by their title of office, i.e. they should be called *Premier* in an address or conversation. Note that a Canadian Premier should not be addressed as Mr./ Ms./Mrs./Mme. Premier, as those are foreign forms of address that are not customary in Canada.

In an informal social setting, the Premier may be addressed as *Mr./Ms./Mrs./Mme. (surname)*, or as *Sir*, or *Ma'am*. A Premier should never be addressed by their first name unless the Premier specifically invites someone to address them in that manner.

Correspondence With a Territorial Premier

Correspondence with a Premier should be addressed as follows:

> The Honourable . . . (Insert the full name and any

other personal post-nominal letters[44])
Premier of the Territory of _____
(Insert address of the Territorial Legislature)

<u>The beginning salutation in a letter:</u>

Dear Premier:

<u>The closing salutation in a letter:</u>

Yours Truly,

59. The Spouse of a Premier of a Territory

The spouse of a territorial Premier is addressed in the same manner as any other Canadian citizen (i.e. *Mr./ M./Ms./Mrs./Mme (surname)*. Where the circumstances are very formal, or there is a great age disparity between the speakers, the spouse of the territorial Premier may be addressed as *Sir* or *Ma'am*.

Correspondence With the Spouse of a Premier of a Territory

Ms./Mrs./Mr. . . . (Insert the name and any personal post-nominal letters, if known)
(Insert the personal address of the recipient)

<u>The beginning salutation in a letter:</u>

Dear Madam:

or

Dear Sir:

<u>The closing salutation in a letter:</u>

Yours Truly,

---

44. Elected members of a territorial legislature do not have official post-nominal letters to denote that status.

60. Former Premiers of a Territory

A former Premier of a Territory does not retain the honourific title of The Honourable once they cease to hold office.

Addressing a former Premier in Person

A former Territorial Premier is an ordinary citizen and subject of the Canadian Sovereign and should be addressed in the same manner as any other Canadian would be addressed in appropriate social contexts. Depending on the circumstances, and the relationship between the speakers, a former Premier should be addressed as, for example, *Mr.* Smith or *Ms.* Smith. Where the circumstances are very formal, or there is a great age disparity between the speakers, the former Premier may be addressed as *Sir* or *Ma'am*.

Correspondence With a Former Premier of a Territory

Mr./Mrs./ Ms./ Mme./. . . (Insert the name and any personal post-nominal letters, if known)

The beginning salutation in a letter:

Dear Sir:

or

Dear Madam:

The closing salutation in a letter:

Yours Truly,

61. The Spouse of a Former Premier of a Territory

The spouse of a former Premier is addressed in the same manner as any other Canadian citizen (i.e. *Mr./ M./Ms./Mrs./Mme* *(surname)*. Where the circumstances are very formal, or there is a great age disparity between the speakers, the spouse of the territorial Premier may be addressed as *Sir* or *Ma'am*.

Correspondence With the Spouse of a Former Premier of a Territory

> Ms./Mrs./Mme./Mr/M. . . . (Insert the name and any personal post-nominal letters, if known)
> (Insert the personal address of the recipient)

> The beginning salutation in a letter:

> *Dear Madam:*

> or

> *Dear Sir:*

> The closing salutation in a letter:

> *Yours Truly,*

62. Territorial Ministers

When appearing before a Minister of a Territory in a formal setting, Canadians should refer to him or her by their title of office, i.e. they should be called *Minister* in an address or conversation. Note that a territorial Minister should not be addressed as Mr./ Ms./Mrs./Mme Minister, as those are foreign forms of address that are not customary in Canada.

In an informal social setting, a Minister may be addressed as *Mr./Ms./Mrs./Mme. (surname)*, or as *Sir,* or *Ma'am*. A Minister should never be addressed by their first name unless the Minister specifically invites someone to address them in that manner.

Correspondence With a Territorial Minister

Correspondence with a Minister should be addressed as follows:

The Honourable . . . (Insert the full name and any
personal post-nominal letters)
Minister of _____
Territory of _____
(Insert address of the Territorial Legislature)

The beginning salutation in a letter:

Dear Minister:

The closing salutation in a letter:

Yours Truly,

THE TERRITORIAL LEGISLATURES

63. The Speaker of a Territorial Legislature

The Speaker of a Territorial Legislature is the presiding officer
of that assembly. He or she enforces the rules for the conduct of
proceedings and adjudicates disputes over parliamentary procedure within the Chamber of the Legislature. The Speaker also
carries out administrative functions concerning the legislature.
The Speaker is elected by the members of the legislature.

Addressing the Speaker of a Territorial Legislature in Person

When appearing before the Speaker of a Territorial Legislature,
Canadians should refer to them as *Madam Speaker*, if the
Speaker is a woman or *Mr. Speaker*, if the incumbent is a man.

In an informal social setting, a Speaker of a Territorial Legislature may be addressed as *Mr./Ms./Mrs./Mme (surname)*, or as *Sir*,
or *Madam*. A Speaker of a Territorial Legislature should never
be addressed by their first name unless the Speaker specifically
invites someone to address them in that manner.

Correspondence with the Speaker of a Territorial Legislature

Correspondence with the Speaker of a Territorial Legislature should be addressed as follows:

> The Honourable (Insert full name) (Insert any personal post-nominal letters)
> Speaker of the _____
> (Insert address of the Territorial Legislature

> The beginning salutation in a letter:

> *Dear Mr. Speaker:*

> or

> *Dear Madam Speaker:*

> The closing salutation in a letter:

> *Yours Truly,*

64. Members of a Territorial Legislature

When appearing before a Member of a Legislature of a Territory in a formal or informal setting, Canadians should refer to him or her as *Mr./ Ms./Mrs./Mme. (surname)* or as *Sir* or *Ma'am* unless invited to address the Member informally.

Correspondence With a Member of a Territorial Legislature

Correspondence with a member of a Territorial Legislature should be addressed as follows:

> Mr./ Ms./ Mrs./Mme. (Insert the full name and any post-nominal letters)
> Member of the Legislative Assembly of _____ (insert territorial name)
> (Insert address of the Territorial Legislature)

The beginning salutation in a letter:

Dear Sir:

or

Dear Madam:

The closing salutation in a letter:

Yours Truly,

THE PUBLIC SERVICES

65. Public Servants

Public or Civil Servants at any level of government in Canada are addressed in the same manner as any other citizen of Canada. There is no special distinction that attaches to them by virtue of their employment. As with private citizens in any business-type meeting, a public servant should be addressed as *Mr./Mrs./Ms./M./Mme. (surname)* unless one is invited by them to use their first name. As a general practice, it is likely that most junior officials will quickly ask you to address them by their first name. More senior officials (e.g. a Deputy Minister) may prefer to be addressed more formally.

Correspondence with Federal, Provincial, Territorial or Local Public Servants

Correspondence with public or civil servants should be addressed as follows:

Ms./Mrs./Mme./Mr./M. . . . (Insert the name and any post-nominal letters)
Insert the job title of the recipient
(Insert the business address of the recipient)

The beginning salutation in a letter:

Dear Madam:

or

Dear Sir:

The closing salutation in a letter:

Yours Truly

or

Yours Sincerely, (where there is an established business relationship between the correspondents)

THE ARMED FORCES

66. Armed Forces Personnel

Members of the Armed Forces should be addressed by their rank in the service to which they belong. This holds true for both in-person interactions and for correspondence.

Correspondence with a Member of the Canadian Armed Forces

Correspondence with a member of the Canadian Armed Forces by civilians should be addressed as follows. For members of the Canadian Armed Forces military protocols should be followed.

(Insert military rank e.g. Colonel . . . . (Insert the name and any post-nominal letters[45])
Insert the military position held by the recipient
(Insert the official address of the recipient)

---

45. In navies that trace their antecedents to Britain's Royal Navy, including the Royal Canadian Navy, it is customary in addressing correspondence to place the abbreviation for the country's naval service after the surname and before any post-nominal letters for officers below the rank of Commodore, i.e. R.C.N. followed by the individual's post-nominal letters.

The beginning salutation in a letter:

Dear (e.g. Colonel) (insert surname):

The closing salutation in a letter:

Yours Truly,

Note: Where a military service member has been appointed as an aide-de-camp to the Sovereign or the Sovereign's representatives in Canada they are entitled to be addressed in correspondence with the post-nominal letters A. de C.

LOCAL GOVERNMENT AND ABORIGINAL FIRST NATIONS

Local governments are the closest form of government to the people of Canada and they administer a wide range of local services to the inhabitants of a community. There are two common forms of local governments in Canada. Firstly, there are municipalities, of various forms, and a multiplicity of names describing such local entities. Municipalities are subject to the jurisdiction of the provinces and territories. Secondly, there are reserves established under the *Indian Act*[46] that provide services to Aboriginal Canadians residing on those reserves. Reserves established under the *Indian Act* are subject to the jurisdiction of the federal government.

67. Mayors

Municipalities come with a variety of structures and names. Where a municipality is designated as a city or town the highest local official will invariably bear the title of Mayor. A Mayor in any of the provinces and territories except Quebec is entitled to the prefix honourific of *Your Worship*.

Addressing a Mayor in Person

46. RSC 1985, c. I-5

When appearing before a Mayor in a formal setting, in all provinces and territories except Quebec Canadians should refer to him or her firstly as *Your Worship* and then by their title of office, i.e. they should subsequently be called *Mayor* in an address or conversation. In Quebec, a Mayor should be addressed simply as *Mayor,* as there is no prefix honourific applicable to mayors in that province. A Mayor should never be addressed by their first name unless the Mayor specifically invites someone to address them in that manner.

In an informal social setting, a Mayor may be addressed as *Mr./M./Ms./Mrs./Mme. (surname),* or as *Sir* or *Ma'am.*

Correspondence With a Mayor

Correspondence with a Mayor of a City or Town should be addressed as follows:

> Her Worship or His Worship[47]. . . (Insert the full name and any personal post-nominal letters, if known)
> Mayor[48] of the (City, Town, Municipality) of
> _____
> (Insert address of the Municipal offices)
>
> The beginning salutation in a letter:
>
> *Dear Sir*
>
> or

47. This form applies to Mayors in all provinces and territories of Canada except the Province of Quebec. The honourific *Your Worship* is not used by Quebec Mayors.
48. In the small community of Niagara on the Lake, Ontario, the first capital of the colony of Upper Canada, which later became Ontario, the head of the municipality is called the Lord Mayor and they should be addressed as such. The title is said to have been conferred by the Duke of Kent in the early nineteenth century to recognize the town's historic importance.

Dear Madam:

or

Your Worship:

The closing salutation in a letter:

Yours Truly,

Correspondence with a Mayor of a City or Town in the Province of Quebec should be addressed as follows:

M./Mme./Mr./Ms./Mrs. (Insert the full name and any personal post-nominal letters)[49]
Mayor of the (City, Town, Municipality) of

––––––––––––––––––

(Insert address of the Municipal offices)

The beginning salutation in (an English) letter:

Dear Sir:

or

Dear Monsieur (surname) :

or

Dear Madame (surname):

The closing salutation in (an English) letter:

Yours Truly,

68. Wardens and Reeves

In the provinces rural municipalities exist that are known as a township or a village. The council of a township or village

49. The honourific "Your Worship" is not used by Quebec Mayors.

may be headed by an official known as a Reeve, who is elected by the inhabitants of a township or village. Several townships and villages may also be included within a larger rural structure known as a County. A County Council is headed by a Warden, who is selected from among the representatives of the various townships and villages included within a County Council.

Addressing a Warden of a County or the Reeve of a Township in Person

When appearing before a Warden or Reeve in a formal setting Canadians should refer to him or her firstly by their title of office, i.e. they should be called *Warden* or *Reeve* in an address or conversation. A Warden or Reeve should never be addressed by their first name unless the person specifically invites someone to address them in that manner.

In an informal social setting, a Warden or Reeve may be addressed as *Mr./M./Ms./Mrs./Mme. (surname)*, or as *Sir* or *Ma'am*.

Correspondence

Correspondence with a Warden of a County or a Reeve of a Township should be addressed as follows:

> Mr./Ms./Mrs./ M./Mme. (Insert the surname and any personal post-nominal letters)
> Warden of the County of _____
>
> or
>
> Reeve of the (Township or Village) of _____)
>
> (insert address of County Offices, or the Township or Village office)
>
> The beginning salutation in a letter:

Dear Sir

or

Dear Madam:

<u>The closing salutation in a letter:</u>

Yours Truly,

69. Members of a Municipal Council

The members of a municipal council are called Councillors. Formerly, in many places, the members of a municipal council were called Alderman and a a few places that name is still used. However, the title Alderman is being phased out in the country because of the impetus to adopt gender-neutral language. The title of Councillor is now the preferred alternative.

Addressing a Member of a Municipal Council

When appearing before a member of a municipal council in a formal or informal setting, Canadians should refer to him or her as *Mr./ Ms./Mrs./Mme. (surname)* or as *Sir* or *Ma'am* unless invited to address the Member informally.

Correspondence

Correspondence with a member of a municipal council should be addressed as follows:

> Ms./Mrs./Mme./Mr./M. . . . (Insert the name and any post-nominal letters)
> Councillor (or Alderman)
> (The City of . . ., Town of . . . , Municipality of . . .)
> (Insert the address of the municipal offices)

<u>The beginning salutation in a letter:</u>

Dear Sir

or

Dear Madam:

The closing salutation in a letter:

Yours Truly,

70. First Nation Reserve Chiefs

Reserves are lands set aside for the aboriginal population of Canada and are governed in local matters by a democratically-elected Band Council established by the federal government under the provisions of the *Indian Act*. There are about 620 such local governments established across Canada and they are collectively described as First Nations. The highest official in each local First Nation government bears the title of Chief. The other members of the Band Council are known as Councillors.

Addressing a Chief of a First Nation Council in Person

When appearing before a Chief of a Band Council in a formal setting Canadians should refer to him or her firstly by their title of office, i.e. they should be called *Chief* in an address or conversation. A Chief should never be addressed by their first name unless the person specifically invites someone to address them in that manner.

In an informal social setting, a Chief may be addressed as *Mr./M./Ms./Mrs./Mme. (surname)*, or as *Sir* or *Ma'am*.

Correspondence

Correspondence with a Chief of a First Nations Band Council should be addressed as follows:

> M./Mme./Mr./Ms./Mrs. (Insert the full name and any personal post-nominal letters)

Chief of the _____ First Nation
(Insert address of the Band Council offices)

The beginning salutation in a letter:

Dear Sir

or

Dear Madam:

or

Dear Chief

The closing salutation in a letter:

Yours Truly,

71. Members of a First Nation Band Council

The members of a band council established under the *Indian Act* are called Councillors.

Addressing a Member of a First Nation Band Council

When appearing before a member of a band council in a formal or informal setting, Canadians should refer to him or her as *Mr./ Ms./Mrs./Mme. (surname)* or as *Sir* or *Ma'am* unless invited to address the Member informally.

Correspondence

Correspondence with a member of a First Nation band council should be addressed as follows:

> Ms./Mrs./Mme./Mr./M. . . . (Insert the name and any post-nominal letters)
> Councillor

(insert the name of the First Nation)
(Insert the address of the band council offices)

The beginning salutation in a letter:

Dear Sir

or

Dear Madam:

The closing salutation in a letter:

Yours Truly,

THE JUDICIARY AND THE LEGAL PROFESSION

The highest court in Canada is the Supreme Court of Canada which is a statutory appellate court established under the *Constitution Act* of 1867. The Supreme Court is the final level of appeal from the provincial Superior Courts on all matters.

Below the Supreme Court are the Superior Courts of the provinces and territories which are the direct successors of the Royal Courts of Justice at Westminster in England. The provincial Superior Courts possess original jurisdiction which means that any claim recognized by law is within the jurisdiction of those courts unless the matter has been excluded. The Superior Courts of the Provinces and Territories hear most civil claims for compensation, or damages, as well as the most serious criminal cases.

Below the level of the Provincial Superior Courts are the so-called inferior courts. Those are the statutory Provincial or Territorial Courts that hear the bulk of criminal law matters, and the bulk of family law cases. Appeals from the Provincial or Territorial Courts may be taken to the Provincial or Territorial Superior Courts.

As an exception to the unitary judicial structure Parliament has created the Federal Court and the Federal Court of Appeal as a statutory Superior Court to hear certain matters that fall exclusively within federal constitutional jurisdiction, primarily in the areas of federal administrative law and admiralty law.

Parliament has also established two other statutory Superior Courts with very specific mandates, the Tax Court, which primarily hears appeals from income tax assessments, and a Court Martial Appeal Court to hear appeals from military courts-martial. Apart from these jurisdictionally narrow federal exceptions, Canada maintains a unitary judicial system although Canada is a federal state.

72. The Chief Justice of Canada

The Supreme Court of Canada is the highest-level judicial tribunal in Canada. It consists of nine Justices appointed by the federal government. One Justice is appointed to be the Chief Justice of Canada and has overall administrative responsibilities in connection with Court operations.

Addressing the Chief Justice of Canada

When appearing before the Chief Justice of Canada in a formal setting outside of the courtroom of the Supreme Court Canadians should refer to him or her firstly by their title of office, i.e. they should be called *Chief Justice* in an address or conversation. Afterwards, they may be addressed as *Sir* or *Madam*. A Chief Justice should never be addressed by their first name unless the person specifically invites someone to address them in that manner.

Addressing the Chief Justice of Canada in Correspondence

The Chief Justice of Canada bears the honourific prefix of *The Right Honourable* for life. A Chief Justice of Canada is invariably summoned to be a member of the King's Privy Council for

Canada. Accordingly, correspondence with the Chief Justice of Canada must reflect that status and should be addressed as follows:

> The Right Honourable ... (Insert full name and the post-nominal letters, P.C., and then other personal post-nominal letters[50])
> Chief Justice of Canada
> Supreme Court of Canada
> Ottawa, ON
> K1A 0J1
>
> The beginning salutation in a letter:
>
> *Dear Chief Justice:*
>
> The closing salutation in a letter:
>
> *Yours Truly,*

73. Justices of the Supreme Court of Canada

When appearing before a Justice of the Supreme Court of Canada in a formal setting outside of the courtroom Canadians should refer to him or her firstly by their title of office and name, i.e. they should be called *Justice (surname)*, in an address or conversation. Afterwards, they may be addressed as *Sir* or *Madam*. A Justice should never be addressed by their first name unless the person specifically invites someone to address them in that manner.

Addressing a Justice of the Supreme Court of Canada in Correspondence

A Justice of the Supreme Court of Canada bears the honourific

---

50. If a judicial appointee has formerly been appointed as a King's Counsel they must surrender or place in abeyance the office of King's Counsel upon taking up a judicial appointment and therefore the post-nominal letters K.C. are omitted.

prefix of *The Honourable* for their entire term of office as a member of the Supreme Court but they lose that designation upon their retirement, or resignation, from the Court unless the Crown grants them the right to continue to use that honourific prefix. A Justice of the Supreme Court of Canada should be addressed in correspondence as follows:

> The Honourable Mr. Justice (Insert surname and any personal post-nominal letters,)
>
> or
>
> The Honourable Madam Justice (Insert surname and any personal post-nominal letters,)
> Supreme Court of Canada
> Ottawa, ON
> K1A 0J1
>
> The beginning salutation in a letter:
>
> *Dear Justice (insert surname):*
>
> The closing salutation in a letter:
>
> *Yours Truly,*

74. The Registrar of the Supreme Court of Canada

The Registrar is the senior administrative officer of the Court and also has responsibility for some quasi-judicial processes in connection with the procedures of the Supreme Court.

Addressing the Registrar of the Supreme Court of Canada

When appearing before the Registrar of the Supreme Court in a formal setting outside of the courtroom of the Supreme Court Canadians should refer to him or her as *Mr.(insert surname)* or *Madam (insert surname).*

Correspondence with the Registrar of the Supreme Court of Canada

Correspondence with the Registrar of the Supreme Court of Canada should be addressed as follows:

> M./Mme./Mr./Ms./Mrs. (Insert the full name and any personal post-nominal letters)
> Registrar,
> Supreme Court of Canada
> Ottawa, ON
> K1A 0J1

The beginning salutation in a letter:

Dear Sir

or

Dear Madam:

The closing salutation in a letter:

Yours Truly,

75. Justices of a Provincial or Territorial Superior Court

When appearing before a Justice of a provincial or territorial Superior Court in a formal setting outside of the courtroom Canadians should refer to him or her firstly by their title of office and name, i.e. they should be called *Justice (surname)*, in an address, or conversation. Afterwards, they may be addressed as *Sir* or *Madam*. A Justice should never be addressed by their first name unless the person specifically invites someone to address them in that manner.

Addressing a Justice of a Provincial or Territorial Superior Court in Correspondence[51]

51. If a judicial appointee has formerly been appointed as a King's Counsel they

A Justice of a provincial or territorial Superior Court bears the honourific prefix of *The Honourable* for their entire term of office as a member of a provincial Superior Court but they lose that designation upon their retirement, or resignation, from a Court unless the Crown grants them the right to continue to use the honourific prefix after they cease to be a judge. Any Justice of a provincial Superior Court in Canada should be addressed in correspondence as follows:

> The Honourable Mr. Justice _____
> (Insert surname and any personal post-nominal letters, if known)

> or

> The Honourable Madam Justice _____ (Insert surname and any personal post-nominal letters, if known)
> (insert the address of the Superior Court)

> The beginning salutation in a letter:

> *Dear Justice (insert surname):*

> or

> The closing salutation in a letter:

> *Yours Truly,*

76. Members of the Federal Court, Federal Court of Appeal, Tax Court of Canada or the Court Martial Appeal Court

When appearing before a Justice of one of the federal courts of Canada in a formal setting outside of the courtroom Canadians should refer to him or her firstly by their title of office and

must surrender or place in abeyance the office of King's Counsel upon taking up a judicial appointment and therefore the post-nominal letters K.C. are omitted.

The manner of addressing judges and judicial officers in Canada has generally followed the British tradition but in recent years, perhaps owing to the the desire for more gender-neutral language the manner of addressing judges in several of the provinces has begun to change.

77. Addressing the Chief Justice of Canada in a Court Proceeding

In a court proceeding the Chief Justice of Canada should be addressed as *Chief Justice*.

78. Addressing a Justice of the Supreme Court of Canada in a Court Proceeding

In a court proceeding a Justice of the Supreme Court of Canada should be addressed as *Justice (insert surname)*

79. Addressing the Registrar of the Supreme Court of Canada in a Court Proceeding

In any court process conducted by the Registrar of the Supreme Court of Canada, the Registrar should be addressed as *Madam Registrar* or *Mr. Registrar.*

80. Addressing a Justice of one of the Federal Courts of Canada in a Court Proceeding

In a court proceeding a Justice of the Federal Court, Federal Court of Appeal, Tax Court of Canada and the Court Martial Appeal Court the Justices should be addressed as *Justice (surname)*

81. Newfoundland and Labrador Courts

1. Supreme Court and Court of Appeal

• *My Lord* or *Your Lordship*

• *My Lady* or *Your Ladyship*

2. Provincial Court

• *Your Honour*

82. Prince Edward Island Courts

1. Supreme Court and Court of Appeal

• *My Lord* or *Your Lordship*

• *My Lady* or *Your Ladyship*

2. Provincial Court

• *Your Honour*

83. Nova Scotia Courts

1. Supreme Court and Court of Appeal

• *My Lord* or *Your Lordship*

• *My Lady* or *Your Ladyship*

2. Provincial Court

• *Your Honour*

84. New Brunswick Courts

1. Court of King's Bench and Court of Appeal

• *Chief Justice* (when he or she presides)

• *Justice*

• *Mr. Justice* _____

• *Madam Justice* _____

2. Provincial Court

- *Your Honour*

85. Quebec Courts

1. Superior Court and Court of Appeal

- *Mr. Justice _____*

- *Madam Justice _____*

2. Provincial Court

- *Judge (surname)*

86. Ontario Courts

1. Court of Appeal

- *Chief Justice* (when present)

- *Justice or Justice (surname)*

2. Superior Court

- *Your Honour*

3. Provincial Court

a) Judges

- *Your Honour*

b) Justices of the Peace

- *Your Worship*

87. Manitoba Courts

1. Court of Appeal

- *My Lord* or *Your Lordship*

- *My Lady* or *Your Ladyship*

2. Court of King's Bench

a) Justices

- *My Lord* or *Your Lordship*

- *My Lady* or *Your Ladyship*

b) Masters

- *Your Honour*

3. Provincial Court

- *Your Honour*

88. Saskatchewan Courts

1. Court of Appeal and Court of King's Bench

- *Chief Justice* (when present)

- *Associate Chief Justice* (when present)

- *Justice or Justice (surname)*

2. Provincial Court

- *Your Honour*

89. Alberta Courts

1. Court of Appeal and Court of King's Bench

- *Chief Justice* (when present)

- *Justice or Justice (surname)*

2. Provincial Court

a) Judges

- *Your Honour*

b) Traffic Commissioners

- *Your Worship*

90. British Columbia Courts

1. Court of Appeal and Supreme Court Justices

- *Chief Justice* (when present)

- *Justice or Justice (surname)*

2. Supreme Court Master

- *Your Honour*

3. Supreme Court Registrar

- *Mr. Registrar or Madam Registrar*

4. Provincial Court

a) Judges

- *Your Honour*

b) Justices of the Peace/Judicial Justices

- *Your Worship*

91. Yukon Courts

1. Court of Appeal

- *My Lord* or *Your Lordship*

- *My Lady* or *Your Ladyship*

2. Supreme Court

- *Your Honour*

3. Territorial Court

a) Judges

- *Your Honour*

b) Justices of the Peace

- *Your Worship*

92. Northwest Territories Courts

1. Court of Appeal and Supreme Court

- *Chief Justice* (when present)

- *Justice or Justice (surname)*

> or

- *Your Honour*

2. Territorial Court

- *Your Honour*

93. Nunavut Courts

1. All Nunavut Courts

- *Mr. Justice (surname)*

- *Madam Justice (surname)*

> or

- *Your Honour*

94. Lawyers

Lawyers are officers of the courts and work to uphold the inviolability of the courts and the judicial process throughout Canada. Historically, in the days of the empire, they were considered part of the gentry classes and ranked and described in correspondence as *Esquires* (or *Esq.*)in the common law jurisdictions within Canada. In Quebec, the advocates and notaries were similarly treated but there they bore the title of *Maître* or Master (abb. *Me.* or *Mtre.*). Today, such titles are unnecessary in general correspondence although they may still used, and they may have greater usage within the legal profession than in relations between the general public and the legal profession.

In Quebec, the title *maître* was applied to both male and female lawyers but in Anglophone Canada, the title of *esquire* was historically an exclusively male title. Thus it was very rare (although not unheard of) for a female Barrister and Solicitor to use this title. Because it was seen to be very much a masculine title it fell out of favour for official purposes even within the legal profession when a great influx of females into the profession occurred in the latter decades of the twentieth century.

The author recalls that the last communication that he received from the Law Society of Upper Canada that used the title of *esquire* came with a receipt for annual professional dues dated December 7, 1989. In a subsequent letter dated April 10, 1990, the Secretary of the Society, Richard F. Tinsley, advised all members that the Law Society had adopted gender-neutral communications stating:

> Gender-based communication reinforces preconceived and limited roles based on feminine and masculine stereotypes. Gender-biased communication includes both gender-biased language and other forms of communication. Unbiased representation of both

sexes accords them equality of stature and recognizes the potential for full participation in society on the basis of ability.[54]

The societal trend away from these customary titles is consistent with the evolution of a more egalitarian Canadian society in the late twentieth and early twenty-first centuries. Although the legal profession now encourages gender-neutral communications it is still acceptable for lawyers to be formally addressed using a traditional titular honourific.

Where a lawyer has been appointed as a King's Counsel they are entitled to the use of the post-nominal letters K.C. after their names and in such cases the title *esquire* is not used.

Addressing a Lawyer in Person

Lawyers may generally be addressed in the same manner as any other citizen of Canada. There is no special distinction that attaches to them by their profession. As with private citizens in any business-type meeting, a lawyer should be addressed as *Mr./Mrs./Ms./M./Mme. (surname)* unless one is invited by them to use their first name.

Addressing a Lawyer in Correspondence

1) Standard – Common law provinces and territories

> Ms./Mrs./Mme./Mr./M. . . . (Insert the name and any post-nominal letters e.g. K.C., if known[55])
> Barrister and Solicitor
> (Insert the business address of the recipient)

The beginning salutation in a letter:

Dear Madam:

---

54. R.F. Tinsley,, *Letter RE Gender Neutral Communications*, Law Society of Upper Canada, Toronto, April 10, 1990.

55. The post-nominal letters K.C. should precede any academic degrees

or

Dear Sir:

The closing salutation in a letter:

Yours Sincerely,

2) Formal in Common Law Provinces and Territories

John Smith, Esq.
Barrister and Solicitor
(Insert mailing address)

Note that the honourific *Mr.* is not used when a person is addressed as an esquire. *Esquire* or *Esq.* is also not used if a lawyer has been appointed as a King's Counsel (K.C.).

3) Standard – Quebec

M./Mme./Mlle./Ms./Mrs./Mr./. . . . (Insert the name and any post-nominal letters e.g. c.r.[56])
Avocat/Notaire
(Insert the business address of the recipient)

The beginning salutation in a letter:

Dear Madam:

or

Dear Sir:

The closing salutation in a letter:

Yours Sincerely,

4) Formal – Quebec

---

56. c.r. for *conseil du roi* is the French rendering of King's Counsel

Me. or Mtre[57] . . . . (Insert the name and any post-nominal letters e.g. c.r.)
Avocat/Notaire
(Insert the business address of the recipient)

The beginning salutation in a letter:

Dear Madam:

or

Dear Sir:

The closing salutation in a letter:

Yours Sincerely,

95. The Diplomatic Corps

The Diplomatic Corps concerns the foreign ambassadors, high commissioners and other representatives of foreign states who are sent to Canada to maintain formal relations between those states and Canada. A High Commissioner is the representative of a Commonwealth country in Canada and an Ambassador is the representative of a non-Commonwealth foreign country. The Nuncio is the diplomatic representative of the Vatican in Canada. Foreign diplomats are accorded by custom the honourific *Your Excellency* or *Excellency* when being addressed.

Addressing an Ambassador, High Commissioner or Nuncio in Person

When appearing before a foreign High Commissioner, Ambassador, or Papal Nuncio to Canada, Canadians should refer to the diplomat as *Your Excellency,* or *Excellency*, and thereafter as *Ma'am*, if the Ambassador or High Commissioner is a woman, or *Sir*, if the Ambassador or High Commissioner is a man. Papal Nuncios accredited to Canada are invariably male.

57. Abbreviations for *maître.*

Addressing an Ambassador, High Commissioner or Nuncio in Correspondence

Correspondence with a foreign Ambassador, High Commissioner or Nuncio stationed or accredited to Canada should be addressed as follows:

(Female foreign Ambassador or High Commissioner)

> Her Excellency. . . (Insert full name and any post-nominal letters, if known)
> Ambassador/High Commissioner of (insert name of foreign or Commonwealth country)
> mailing address (Insert address of diplomatic post serving Canada)

or

(Male foreign Ambassador or High Commissioner)

> His Excellency. . . (Insert full name and any post-nominal letters, if known)
> Ambassador/High Commissioner of (insert name of foreign or Commonwealth country)
> mailing address (Insert address of diplomatic post serving Canada)

or

(Papal Nuncio)

> His Excellency The Most Reverend (insert full name and post-nominal letters, if known)
> Insert religious title (e.g. Monsignor, Archbishop etc.)
> Apostolic Nuncio
> mailing address (Insert address of diplomatic post serving Canada)

The above text applies only to foreign diplomats stationed or accredited in Canada. When Canadians speak to, or correspond with a Canadian diplomat they should not address them as Your Excellency or Excellency. Canadian diplomats are addressed by Canadians in the same way as any other Canadian public servant (see above under Public Services). If engaging with them abroad in the country to which they are accredited they may be addressed as *Ma'am*, if the Ambassador or High Commissioner is a woman, or *Sir*, if the Ambassador or High Commissioner is a man.

APPENDIX A - PRECEDENCE OF REGIMENTS OF THE CANADIAN ARMY

The precedence of organized regiments and units of the Canadian Army is as follows:

A. Armoured Regiments – Regular Force

1. The Royal Canadian Dragoons.
2. Lord Strathcona's Horse (Royal Canadians).
3. 12e Régiment blindé du Canada

<u>Armoured Regiments – Primary Reserve</u>

1. The Governor General's Horse Guards.
2. 8th Canadian Hussars.
3. The Halifax Rifles (RCAC).
4. The Ontario Regiment (RCAC).
5. The Queen's York Rangers (1st American Regiment) (RCAC).
6. The Sherbrooke Hussars.
7. 8th Canadian Hussars (Princess Louise's).
8. 12e Régiment blindé du Canada (Milice)*.
9. 1st Hussars.
10. The Prince Edward Island Regiment (RCAC).
11. The Royal Canadian Hussars (Montreal).
12. The British Columbia Regiment (Duke of Connaught's Own).
13. The South Alberta Light Horse.
14. The Saskatchewan Dragoons.
15. The King's Own Calgary Regiment
16. The British Columbia Dragoons. (RCAC).
17. The Fort Garry Horse.

name, i.e. they should be called *Justice (insert surname)*[52], in an address or conversation. Afterwards, they may be addressed as *Sir* or *Madam*. A Justice or Judge should never be addressed by their first name unless the person specifically invites someone to address them in that manner.

Addressing a Justice one of the Federal Courts of Canada in Correspondence

A Justice of a Federal Court bears the honourific prefix of *The Honourable* for their entire term of office as a member of a Court but loses that designation upon their retirement or resignation from the Court unless the Crown grants them the right to continue to use the honourific prefix. A Justice of one of the federal courts of Canada should be addressed in correspondence as follows:

> The Honourable Justice (insert surname and any personal post-nominal letters[53])

> (insert the address of the court to which the Justice belongs)

> The beginning salutation in a letter:

> *Dear Justice (insert surname):*

> The closing salutation in a letter:

> *Yours Truly,*

JUDGES AND JUDICIAL OFFICERS IN THE COURTROOM

52. Use "Chief Justice" in place of "Justice" when speaking to the Chief Justice of a federal court.

53. If a judicial appointee has formerly been appointed as a King's Counsel they must surrender or place in abeyance the office of King's Counsel upon taking up a judicial appointment and therefore the post-nominal letters K.C. are omitted.

18. Le Régiment de Hull (RCAC).
19. The Windsor Regiment (RCAC).

<u>Armoured Regiments – Supplementary Reserve</u>

1. 4th Princess Louise Dragoon Guards.
2. 12th Manitoba Dragoons.
3. 19th Alberta Dragoons.
4. 14th Canadian Hussars.

B. Artillery Regiments

1. Horse artillery.
2. Field artillery.
3. Medium artillery.
4. Heavy artillery.
5. Surface-to-surface missile artillery.
6. Anti-tank artillery.
7. Locating artillery (target acquisition).
8. Coast artillery.
9. Mountain artillery.
10. Air defence artillery (guns).
11. Air defence artillery (missile).
12. Regimental headquarters.
13. The Royal Regiment of Canadian Artillery School.

C. Infantry Regiments – Regular Force

1. The Royal Canadian Regiment
2. Princess Patricia's Canadian Light Infantry.
3. Royal 22e Régiment

<u>Infantry Regiments – Primary Reserve</u>

1. Governor General's Foot Guards.
2. The Canadian Grenadier Guards.
3. The Queen's Own Rifles of Canada.
4. The Black Watch (Royal Highland Regiment) of Canada.

5. Les Voltigeurs de Québec.

6. The Royal Regiment of Canada.

7. The Royal Hamilton Light Infantry (Wentworth Regiment).

8. The Princess of Wales' Own Regiment.

9. The Hastings and Prince Edward Regiment.

10. The Lincoln and Welland Regiment.

11. The Royal Canadian Regiment*.

12. The Royal Highland Fusiliers of Canada.

13. The Grey and Simcoe Foresters.

14. The Lorne Scots (Peel, Dufferin and Halton Regiment).

15. The Brockville Rifles.

16. Stormont, Dundas and Glengarry Highlanders.

17. Les Fusiliers du St-Laurent.

18. Le Régiment de la Chaudière.

19. Royal 22e Régiment*.

20. Les Fusiliers Mont-Royal.

21. The Princess Louise Fusiliers.

22. The Royal New Brunswick Regiment.

23. The West Nova Scotia Regiment.

24. The Nova Scotia Highlanders.

25. Le Régiment de Maisonneuve.

26. The Cameron Highlanders of Ottawa.

27. The Royal Winnipeg Rifles.

28. The Essex and Kent Scottish.

29. 48th Highlanders of Canada.

30. Le Régiment du Saguenay.

31. The Algonquin Regiment.

32. The Argyll and Sutherland Highlanders of Canada (Princess Louise's).

33. The Lake Superior Scottish Regiment.

34. The North Saskatchewan Regiment.

35. The Royal Regina Rifles.

36. The Rocky Mountain Rangers.

37. The Loyal Edmonton Regiment (4th Battalion, Princess Patricia's Canadian Light Infantry)

38. The Queen's Own Cameron Highlanders of Canada.

39. The Royal Westminster Regiment.

40. The Calgary Highlanders.

41. Les Fusiliers de Sherbrooke.

42. The Seaforth Highlanders of Canada.

43. The Canadian Scottish Regiment (Princess Mary's).

44. The Royal Montreal Regiment.

45. Irish Regiment of Canada.

46. The Toronto Scottish Regiment (Queen Elizabeth The Queen Mother's Own).

47. The Royal Newfoundland Regiment.

Infantry Regiments – Supplementary Reserve

1. The Canadian Guards

2. Victoria Rifles of Canada.

3. The Royal Rifles of Canada.

4. The Perth Regiment.

5. Le Régiment de Joliette.

6. The Winnipeg Grenadiers.

7. The South Saskatchewan Regiment.

8. The Yukon Regiment.

APPENDIX B - SPECIAL CASES INVOLVING THE DESCRIPTION OF THE SOVEREIGN IN FEDERAL - PROVINCIAL AGREEMENTS

Canada is a federal state, which means that the legal sovereignty of the country is divided between the federal government and the provincial governments. The Sovereign is the head of state for both Canada as a whole and for each of the ten provinces of Canada. When it is necessary in a formal agreement between the federal government and a provincial government to distinguish between the Sovereign, acting in the capacity of the head of state of Canada, and the Sovereign acting in the capacity of the head of state of a province, a special title is used. In such cases, the words "in Right of" and the name of the country or the province are added to the reference to the Sovereign to distinguish in which capacities the Sovereign is acting. For example, when it is necessary to formally refer to the Sovereign acting for and on behalf of the Federal Government the formula used is:

"His Majesty the King in Right of Canada"

Similarly, for each of the provinces, this special formula would be used. Thus, in the present reign, the Sovereign acting on behalf of a Province of Canada would be described in an intergovernmental agreement as:

"His Majesty the King in Right of Ontario"
"His Majesty the King in Right of Quebec"
"His Majesty the King in Right of Nova Scotia"
"His Majesty the King in Right of New Brunswick"
"His Majesty the King in Right of Manitoba"

"His Majesty the King in Right of British Columbia"
"His Majesty the King in Right of Prince Edward Island"
"His Majesty the King in Right of Saskatchewan"
"His Majesty the King in Right of Alberta"
"His Majesty the King in Right of Newfoundland and Labrador"

If a female is enthroned, the description would read "Her Majesty the Queen in Right of Canada," or in right of one or another of the provinces as shown above.

These descriptions are not always necessary in the case of intergovernmental agreements, particularly where there is no intention on the part of either government to create a binding relationship. In many cases, the organs of government are described more informally by descriptions such as "the Government of Canada" or "the Government of [insert name of province]." In other cases, the intergovernmental agreement is described as one between Ministers of the Crown. In such cases, the descriptions used would be "the Minister of [e.g. Immigration]" and the "Minister of [insert provincial Minister's title]." Although informal agreements are not necessarily intended to create legally binding relationships they are still backed by the full faith and honour of the Crown at each level of government, and so invariably they are carried out by each level of government according to the terms of the agreement. However, particularly where a more binding relationship may be intended, the preferred formula is to refer to the Sovereign in right of Canada or in right of a province.

In the case of the Territorial governments, the formal expression "His Majesty in Right of" a territory is not used because the territories of Canada do not possess a sovereign status under the *Constitution Act, 1867*, and therefore they remain constitutionally subordinate to the federal government. Nevertheless, as a practical matter, the territories operate at arms-length from the federal government, with devolved responsibilities and so it is natural for the territories, like their provincial counterparts, to enter into intergovernmental arrangements with the federal government. In such cases, the two governments would normally use the more informal descriptions of "Government of Canada" and Government of [territory]" to regulate the arrangements they propose to make.

APPENDIX C - MAILING ADDRESSES OF THE OFFICES OF THE LIEUTENANT GOVERNORS OF CANADIAN PROVINCES

Alberta

The Lieutenant Governor of Alberta
3rd Floor, Legislature Building
10800 – 97 Avenue
Edmonton, Alberta T5K 2B6

British Columbia

The Lieutenant Governor of British Columbia
Government House
1401 Rockland Avenue
Victoria, B.C. V8S IV9

Manitoba

The Lieutenant Governor of Manitoba
Room 235 Legislative Building
Winnipeg, MB R3C 0V8

New Brunswick

The Lieutenant Governor of New Brunswick
Government House
P. O. Box 6000
Fredericton, NB
E3B 5H1

Newfoundland and Labrador

The Lieutenant Governor of Newfoundland and Labrador
Government House
P.O. Box 5517
St. John's, NL
A1C 5W4

Nova Scotia

The Lieutenant Governor of Nova Scotia
Government House
1451 Barrington Street
Halifax, Nova Scotia, B3J 1Z2

Ontario

The Lieutenant Governor of Ontario
Queen's Park
Toronto, Ontario M7A 1A1

Prince Edward Island

The Lieutenant Governor of Prince Edward Island
Government House
P.O. Box 846
Charlottetown PE C1A 7L9

Quebec

The Lieutenant Governor of Québec
Édifice André-Laurendeau, RC
1050, rue des Parlementaires
Québec (Québec) G1A 1A1

Saskatchewan

The Lieutenant Governor of Saskatchewan
Government House
4607 Dewdney Avenue
Regina, SK S4T 1B7

APPENDIX D - MAILING ADDRESSES OF THE OFFICES OF THE COMMISSIONERS OF CANADIAN TERRITORIES

Office of the Commissioner of the Northwest Territories
P.O. Box 1320
803 Northwest Tower
Yellowknife, NT X1A 2L9

Office of the Commissioner of Nunavut
2554 Paurngaq Cres.
Iqaluit NU
X0A 2H0

Commissioner of Yukon
412 Main Street
Whitehorse, Yukon Y1A 2B7

SELECT BIBLIOGRAPHY

Books

Fox-Davies, Arthur Charles, A Complete Guide to Heraldry, Gramercy Books, New York/Avenel (New Jersey), 1993

Hickey, Robert, Honor & Respect, The Official Guide to Names, Titles & Forms of Address, The Protocol School of Washington, Columbia (South Carolina), 2008

Lordon, Paul, Q.C., Crown Law, Butterworths, Toronto and Vancouver, 1991

Montague-Smith, Patrick, Debrett's Correct Form, Debrett's Peerage Limited/Headline Book Publishing PLC, London, 1992

McCreery, Christopher, The Canadian Honours System, Dundurn Press, Toronto, 2005

McCreery, Christopher, The Canadian Honours System, Second Edition, Dundurn Press, Toronto,2015

Noonan, Peter W., The Crown and Constitutional Law, Second Edition, Magistralis, Ottawa, 2017

Author unknown, The Canadian Heraldic Authority, Rideau Hall, Ottawa, 1990

Squibb, G.D., Precedence in England and Wales, Clarendon Press, Oxford, 1981

Squibb, G.D., The High Court of Chivalry, A Study of the Civil Law in England, Clarendon Press, Oxford, 1959

Stacey, C.P. (ed.), Historical Documents of Canada, Volume V, The

Arts of War and Peace 1914-1945, Macmillan of Canada, Toronto, 1972

Stokes, Anthony, A View of the Constitution of the British Colonies in North-America and the West Indies, Anthony Stokes, London, 1783

Todd, Alpheus, Parliamentary Government in the British Colonies, London, Longman, Green & Co., 1880

Official Papers

Report of the Standing Committee on Canadian Heritage, Review of National Protocol Procedures, 41st Parliament, 1st Session, October 2012

The Heritage Structure of the Canadian Forces, Department of National Defence, Ottawa, 1999

Official Reports of Debate (Hansard), Legislative Assembly of Ontario

Internet Sources

Internet sources used in this work included Government of Canada websites particularly the sites for the Department of Canadian Heritage, and the Department of National Defence, both of which provided useful information about the topic of precedence in Canada. The Department of Canadian Heritage also provided suggestions on forms of address and I have adopted some of the suggestions offered there. The website of the Department of Justice was consulted for the text of federal statutes.

The Government website of each province and territory was also accessed for information on precedence at the provincial and territorial level and for suggestions around particular forms of address.

For general reference purposes the websites of Wikipedia, The Canadian Encyclopaedia, the Encyclopaedia Britannica, and Alchetron, The Free Social Encyclopedia, have been consulted.

ABOUT THE AUTHOR

Peter W. Noonan joined the Public Service of Canada in 1981 and for the next thirty years, he served as legal counsel to various federal agencies, appearing on their behalf at public hearings and occasionally in the higher courts. Later in his career, he served as a legal advisor in the Department of Justice in Ottawa from whence he retired in 2011.

www.ingramcontent.com/pod-product-compliance
Lightning Source LLC
Chambersburg PA
CBHW041710260326
41914CB00028B/1671